2

HANDS-ON

STEAM

| Science | Technology | Engineering | Arts | Mathematics |

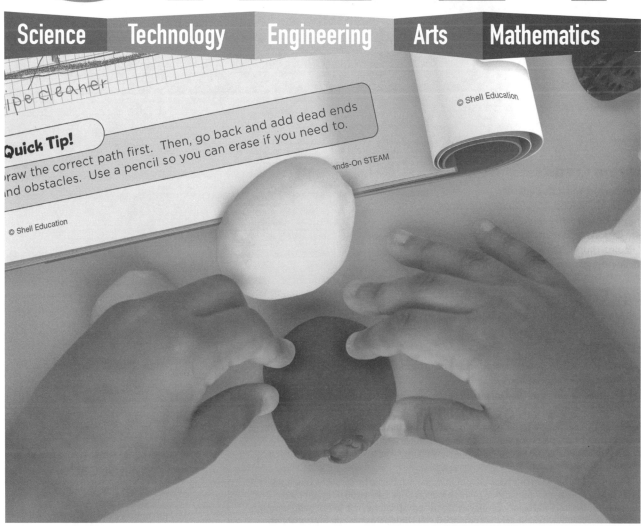

Melissa Laughlin

Program Credits

Corinne Burton, M.A.Ed., *Publisher*
Emily R. Smith, M.A.Ed., *VP of Content Development*
Véronique Bos, *Creative Director*
Lynette Ordoñez, *Content Manager*
Jill Malcolm, *Graphic Designer*
David Slayton, *Assistant Editor*

Image Credits

p.23 Jill Malcolm; all other images Shutterstock and/or iStock

Standards

NGSS Lead States. 2013. *Next Generation Science Standards: For States, By States*. Washington, DC: The National Academies Press.
© 2021 TESOL International Association
© 2021 Board of Regents of the University of Wisconsin System

A division of Teacher Created Materials
5482 Argosy Avenue
Huntington Beach, CA 92649
www.tcmpub.com/shell-education
ISBN 978-1-4258-2529-4
© 2022 Shell Educational Publishing, Inc.
Printed in USA. WOR004

Table of Contents

Introduction

180 Days of Practice

Physical Science

Life Science

Earth Science

Appendixes

Research

The Importance of STEAM Education

STEAM education is a powerful approach to learning that continues to gain momentum and support across the globe. STEAM is the integration of science, technology, engineering, the arts, and mathematics to design solutions for real-world problems. Students must learn how to question, explore, and analyze natural phenomena. With these skills in hand, students understand the complexity of available information and are empowered to become independent learners and problem solvers.

The content and practices of STEAM education are strong components of a balanced instructional approach, ensuring students are college- and career-ready. The application of STEAM practices in the classroom affords teachers opportunities to challenge students to apply new knowledge. Students of all ages can design and build structures, improve existing products, and test innovative solutions to real-world problems. STEAM instruction can be as simple as using recycled materials to design a habitat for caterpillars discovered on the playground and as challenging as designing a solution to provide clean water to developing countries. The possibilities are endless.

Blending arts principles with STEM disciplines prepares students to be problem solvers, creative collaborators, and thoughtful risk-takers. Even students who do not choose a career in a STEAM field will benefit because these skills can be translated into almost any career. Students who become STEAM proficient are prepared to answer complex questions, investigate global issues, and develop solutions for real-world challenges. Rodger W. Bybee (2013, 64) summarizes what is expected of students as they join the workforce:

> As literate adults, individuals should be competent to understand STEM-related global issues; recognize scientific from other nonscientific explanations; make reasonable arguments based on evidence; and, very important, fulfill their civic duties at the local, national, and global levels.

Likewise, STEAM helps students understand how concepts are connected as they gain proficiency in the Four Cs: creativity, collaboration, critical thinking, and communication.

Research *(cont.)*

Defining STEAM

STEAM is an integrated way of preparing students for the twenty-first century world. It places an emphasis on understanding science and mathematics while learning engineering skills. By including art, STEAM recognizes that the creative aspect of any project is integral to good design—whether designing an experiment or an object.

Science

Any project or advancement builds on prior science knowledge. Science focuses on learning and applying specific content, cross-cutting concepts, and scientific practices that are relevant to the topic or project.

Technology

This is what results from the application of scientific knowledge and engineering. It is something that is created to solve a problem or meet a need. Some people also include the *use* of technology in this category. That is, tools used by scientists and engineers to solve problems. In addition to computers and robots, technology can include nets used by marine biologists, anemometers used by meteorologists, computer software used by mathematicians, and so on.

Engineering

This is the application of scientific knowledge to meet a need, solve a problem, or address phenomena. For example, engineers design bridges to withstand huge loads. Engineering is also used to understand phenomena, such as in designing a way to test a hypothesis. When problems arise, such as those due to earthquakes or rising sea levels, engineering is required to design solutions to the problems. On a smaller scale, a homeowner might want to find a solution to their basement flooding.

Art

In this context, art equals creativity and creative problem-solving. For example, someone might want to test a hypothesis but be stumped as to how to set up the experiment. Perhaps you have a valuable painting. You think there is another valuable image below the first layer of paint on the canvas. You do not want to destroy the painting on top. A creative solution is needed. Art can also include a creative or beautiful design that solves a problem. For example, the Golden Gate Bridge is considered both an engineering marvel and a work of art.

Mathematics

This is the application of mathematics to real-world problems. Often, this includes data analysis—such as collecting data, graphing it, analyzing the data, and then communicating that analysis. It may also include taking mathematical measurements in the pursuit of an answer. The idea is not to learn new math, but rather to apply it; however, some mathematics may need to be learned to solve the specific problem. Isaac Newton, for example, is famous for *inventing* calculus to help him solve problems in understanding gravity and motion.

Research *(cont.)*

The Engineering Design Process

The most essential component of STEAM education is the engineering design process. This process is an articulated approach to problem solving in which students are guided through the iterative process of solving problems and refining solutions to achieve the best possible outcomes. There are many different versions of the engineering design process, but they all have the same basic structure and goals. As explained in Appendix I of NGSS (2013), "At any stage, a problem-solver can redefine the problem or generate new solutions to replace an idea that just isn't working out."

Each unit in this resource presents students with a design challenge in an authentic and engaging context. The practice pages guide and support students through the engineering design process to solve problems or fulfill needs.

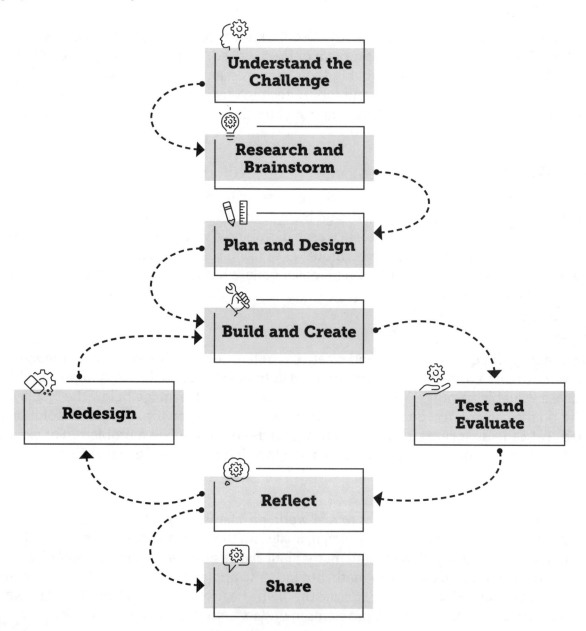

Research *(cont.)*

How to Facilitate Successful STEAM Challenges

There are some basic rules to remember as your students complete STEAM challenges.

Both independent and collaborative work should be included.

Astronaut and inventor Ellen Ochoa is well-known for working a robotic arm in space. About that experience she said, "It's fun to work the robotic arm, in part because it's a team effort." She recognized that she was getting credit for something amazing that happened because of the collaborative work of hundreds of people.

Students need time to think through a project, both on their own and together with others. It is often best to encourage students to start by thinking independently. One student may think of a totally different solution than another student. Once they come together, students can merge aspects of each other's ideas to devise something even better.

Failure is a step in the process.

During the process of trying to invent a useful light bulb, Thomas Edison famously said, "I have not failed. I've just found 10,000 ways that won't work." People are innovating when they are failing because it is a chance to try something new. The STEAM challenges in this book intentionally give students chances to improve their designs. Students should feel free to innovate as much as possible, especially the first time around. Then, they can build on what they learned and try again.

Some students get stuck thinking there is one right way. There are almost always multiple solutions to a problem. For example, attaching train cars together used to be very dangerous. In the late nineteenth century, different solutions to this problem were invented in England and the United States to make the process safer. Both solutions worked, and both were used! Encourage students to recognize that there are usually different ways to solve problems. Discuss the pros and cons of the various solutions that students generate.

Research *(cont.)*

How to Facilitate Successful STEAM Challenges *(cont.)*

Getting inspiration from others is an option.

Students worry a lot about copying. It is important to remind them that all breakthroughs come on the shoulders of others. No one is working in a vacuum, and it is okay to get inspiration and ideas from others. It is also important to give credit to the people whose work and ideas inspired others. Students may see this as cheating, but they should be encouraged to see that they had a great enough idea that others recognized it and wanted to build on it.

The struggle is real—and really important.

Most people do not like to fail. And it can be frustrating not to know what to do or what to try next. Lonnie Johnson, engineer and toy inventor, advises, "Persevere. That's what I always say to people. There's no easy route." Try to support students during this struggle, as amazing innovations can emerge from the process. Further, students feel great when they surprise themselves with success after thinking they were not going to succeed.

Materials can inspire the process.

Students may be stumped about how they are going to build a boat…until you show them that they can use clay. A parachute is daunting, but a pile of tissue paper or plastic bags might suddenly make students feel like they have some direction. On the other hand, materials can also instantly send the mind in certain directions, without exploring other options. For this reason, consider carefully the point at which you want to show students the materials they can use. You might want them to brainstorm materials first. This might inspire you to offer materials you had not considered before.

Some students or groups will need different types of support.

If possible, have students who need additional support manipulate materials, play with commercial solutions, or watch videos to get ideas. For students who need an additional challenge, consider ways to make the challenge more "real world" by adding additional realistic criteria. Or, encourage students to add their own criteria.

How to Use This Resource

Unit Structure Overview

This resource is organized into 12 units. Each three-week unit is organized in a consistent format for ease of use.

Week 1: STEAM Content

Day 1 **Learn Content**	Students read text, study visuals, and answer multiple-choice questions.
Day 2 **Learn Content**	Students read text, study visuals, and answer short-answer questions.
Day 3 **Explore Content**	Students engage in hands-on activities, such as scientific investigations, mini building challenges, and drawing and labeling diagrams.
Day 4 **Get Creative**	Students use their creativity, imaginations, and artistic abilities in activities such as drawing, creating fun designs, and doing science-related crafts.
Day 5 **Analyze Data**	Students analyze and/or create charts, tables, maps, and graphs.

Week 2: STEAM Challenge

Day 1 **Understand the Challenge**	Students are introduced to the STEAM Challenge. They review the criteria and constraints for successful designs.
Day 2 **Research and Brainstorm**	Students conduct additional research, as needed, and brainstorm ideas for their designs.
Day 3 **Plan and Design**	Students plan and sketch their designs.
Day 4 **Build and Create**	Students use their materials to construct their designs.
Day 5 **Test and Evaluate**	Students conduct tests and/or evaluations to assess the effectiveness of their designs and how well they met the criteria of the challenge.

Week 3: STEAM Challenge Improvement

Day 1 **Reflect**	Students answer questions to reflect on their first designs and make plans for how to improve their designs.
Day 2 **Redesign**	Students sketch new or modified designs.
Day 3 **Rebuild and Refine**	Students rebuild or adjust their designs.
Day 4 **Retest**	Students retest and evaluate their new designs.
Day 5 **Reflect and Share**	Students reflect on their experiences working through the engineering design process. They discuss and share their process and results with others.

How to Use This Resource *(cont.)*

Pacing Options

This resource is flexibly designed and can be used in tandem with a core curriculum within a science, STEAM, or STEM block. It can also be used in makerspaces, after-school programs, summer school, or as enrichment activities at home. The following pacing options show suggestions for how to use this book.

Option 1

This option shows how each unit can be completed in 15 days. This option requires approximately 10–20 minutes per day. Building days are flexible, and teachers may allow for additional time at their discretion.

	Day 1	**Day 2**	**Day 3**	**Day 4**	**Day 5**
Week 1	Learn Content	Learn Content	Explore Content	Get Creative	Analyze Data
Week 2	Understand the Challenge	Research and Brainstorm	Plan and Design	Build and Create	Test and Evaluate
Week 3	Reflect	Redesign	Rebuild and Refine	Retest	Reflect and Share

Option 2

This option shows how each unit can be completed in fewer than 15 days. This option requires approximately 45–60 minutes a day.

	Day 1	**Day 2**
Week 1	Learn Content Explore Content	Get Creative Analyze Data
Week 2	Understand the Challenge Research and Brainstorm Plan and Design	Build and Create Test and Evaluate
Week 3	Reflect Redesign Rebuild and Refine	Retest Reflect and Share

How to Use This Resource *(cont.)*

Teaching Support Pages

Each unit in this resource begins with two teaching support pages that provide instructional guidance.

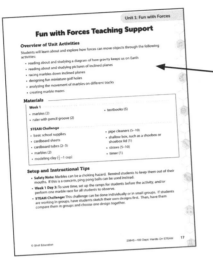

A clear overview of unit activities, weekly materials, safety notes, and setup tips help teachers plan and prepare efficiently and with ease.

Discussion questions help students verbalize their learning and connect it to their own lives.

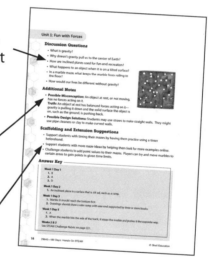

Possible student misconceptions and design solutions help take the guesswork out of lesson planning.

Differentiation options offer ways to support and extend student learning.

Materials

Due to the nature of engineering, the materials listed are often flexible. They may be substituted or added to, depending on what you have available. More material options require greater consideration by students and encourage more creative and critical thinking. Fewer material options can help narrow students' focus but may limit creativity. Adjust the materials provided to fit the needs of your students.

Approximate amounts of materials are included in each list. These amount suggestions are per group. Students are expected to have basic school supplies for each unit. These include paper, pencils, markers or crayons, glue, tape, and scissors.

How to Use This Resource *(cont.)*

Student Pages

Students begin each unit by learning about and exploring science-related content.

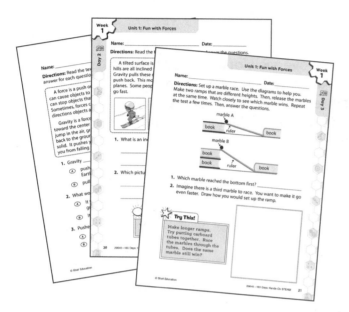

Activities in **Week 1** help build background science content knowledge relevant to the STEAM Challenge.

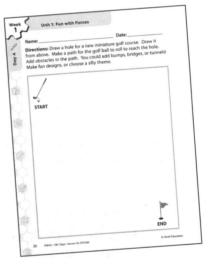

Creative activities encourage students to connect science and art.

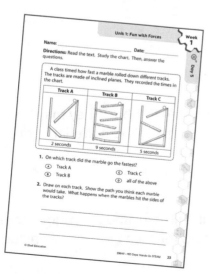

Graphs, charts, and maps guide students to make important mathematics and real-world connections.

How to Use This Resource *(cont.)*

Student Pages *(cont.)*

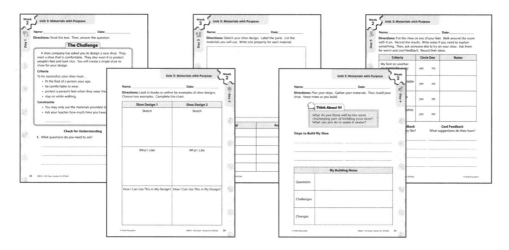

Week 2 introduces students to the STEAM Challenge. Activities guide students through each step of the engineering design process. They provide guiding questions and space for students to record their plans, progress, results, and thinking.

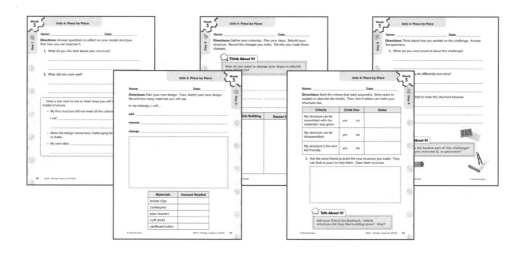

Week 3 activities continue to lead students through the cycle of the engineering design process. Students are encouraged to think about and discuss ways to improve their designs based on their observations and experiences in Week 2.

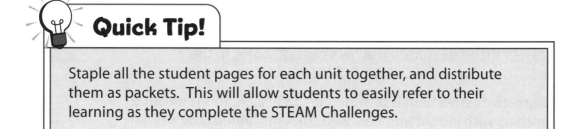

Quick Tip!

Staple all the student pages for each unit together, and distribute them as packets. This will allow students to easily refer to their learning as they complete the STEAM Challenges.

How to Use This Resource *(cont.)*

Assessment Options

Assessments guide instructional decisions and improve student learning. This resource offers balanced assessment opportunities. The assessments require students to think critically, respond to text-dependent questions, and utilize science and engineering practices.

Progress Monitoring

There are key points throughout each unit when valuable formative evaluations can be made. These evaluations can be based on group, paired, and/or individual discussions and activities.

- **Week 1** activities provide opportunities for students to answer multiple-choice and short-answer questions related to the content. Answer keys for these pages are provided in the Teaching Support pages.

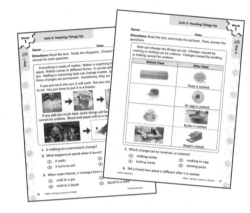

- **Talk About It!** graphics on student activity sheets offer opportunities to monitor student progress.

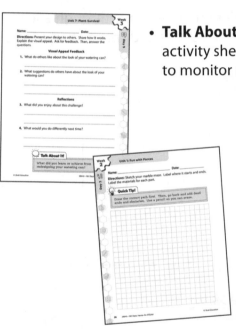

- **Week 2 Day 3: Plan and Design** is when students sketch their first designs. This is a great opportunity to assess how well students understand the STEAM challenge and what they plan to create. These should be reviewed before moving on to the Build and Create stages of the STEAM Challenges.

Summative Assessment

A rubric for the STEAM Challenges is provided on page 221. It is important to note that whether students' final designs were successful is not the main goal of this assessment. It is a way to assess students' skills as they work through the engineering design process. Students assess themselves first. Teachers can add notes to the assessments.

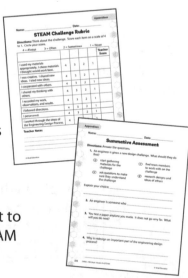

A short summative assessment is provided on page 222. This is meant to provide teachers with insight into how well students understand STEAM practices and the engineering design process.

Standards Correlations

Shell Education is committed to producing educational materials that are research and standards based. To support this effort, this resource is correlated to the academic standards of all 50 states, the District of Columbia, the Department of Defense Dependent Schools, and the Canadian provinces. A correlation is also provided for key professional educational organizations.

To print a customized correlation report for your state, visit our website at **www.tcmpub.com/administrators/correlations** and follow the online directions. If you require assistance in printing correlation reports, please contact the Customer Service Department at 1-800-858-7339.

Standards Overview

The Every Student Succeeds Act (ESSA) mandates that all states adopt challenging academic standards that help students meet the goal of college and career readiness. While many states already adopted academic standards prior to ESSA, the act continues to hold states accountable for detailed and comprehensive standards. Standards are designed to focus instruction and guide adoption of curricula. They define the knowledge, skills, and content students should acquire at each level. Standards are also used to develop standardized tests to evaluate students' academic progress. State standards are used in the development of our resources, so educators can be assured they meet state academic requirements.

Next Generation Science Standards

This set of national standards aims to incorporate science knowledge and process standards into a cohesive framework. The standards listed on page 16 describe the science content and processes presented throughout the lessons.

TESOL and WIDA Standards

In this book, the following English language development standards are met: Standard 1: English language learners communicate for social and instructional purposes within the school setting. Standard 3: English language learners communicate information, ideas and concepts necessary for academic success in the content area of mathematics. Standard 4: English language learners communicate information, ideas and concepts necessary for academic success in the content area of science.

Standards Correlations *(cont.)*

Each unit in this resource supports the following NGSS Scientific and Engineering Practices and Engineering Performance Expectations for K–2.

Scientific and Engineering Practices	Engineering Performance Expectations
Asking Questions and Defining Problems	Ask questions, make observations, and gather information about a situation people want to change to define a simple problem that can be solved through the development of a new or improved object or tool.
Developing and Using Models	
Planning and Carrying Out Investigations	
Analyzing and Interpreting Data	Develop a simple sketch, drawing, or physical model to illustrate how the shape of an object helps it function as needed to solve a given problem.
Constructing Explanations and Designing Solutions	
Engaging in Argument from Evidence	Analyze data from tests of two objects designed to solve the same problem to compare the strengths and weaknesses of how each performs.
Obtaining, Evaluating, and Communicating Information	

This chart shows how the units in this resource align to NGSS Disciplinary Core Ideas and Crosscutting Concepts.

Unit	Disciplinary Core Idea	Crosscutting Concept
Fun with Forces	PS2.A: Forces and Motion	Cause and Effect; Patterns
Heating Things Up	PS1.A: Structure and Properties of Matter PS1.B: Chemical Reactions	Cause and Effect; Patterns
Materials with Purpose	PS1.A: Structure and Properties of Matter	Cause and Effect; Patterns
Piece by Piece	PS1.A: Structure and Properties of Matter	Cause and Effect; Energy and Matter; Patterns
Biodiversity	LS4.D: Biodiversity and Humans	Cause and Effect
Life Cycle of Frogs	LS1.B: Growth and Development of Organisms	Cause and Effect; Patterns; Structure and Function
Plant Survival	LS2.A: Interdependent Relationships in Ecosystems	Patterns; Structure and Function
Pollination Partners	LS2.A: Interdependent Relationships in Ecosystems	Cause and Effect
Erosion	ESS2.A: Earth Materials and Systems ESS1.C: The History of Planet Earth	Stability and Change; Patterns
Maps	ESS2.B: Plate Tectonics and Large-Scale System Interactions	Patterns
Water Cycle	ESS2.C: The Roles of Water in Earth's Surface Processes	Patterns
Volcanoes	ESS2.B: Plate Tectonics and Large-Scale System Interactions ESS1.C: The History of Planet Earth	Cause and Effect; Patterns; Stability and Change

Fun with Forces Teaching Support

Overview of Unit Activities

Students will learn about and explore how forces can move objects through the following activities:

- reading about and studying a diagram of how gravity keeps us on Earth
- reading about and studying pictures of inclined planes
- racing marbles down inclined planes
- designing fun miniature golf holes
- analyzing the movement of marbles on different tracks
- creating marble mazes

Materials Per Group

Week 1

- marbles (2)
- ruler with pencil groove (2)

- textbooks (5)

STEAM Challenge

- basic school supplies
- cardboard sheets
- cardboard tubes (2–3)
- marbles (2)
- modeling clay

- pipe cleaners (5–10)
- shallow box, such as a shoebox or shoebox lid (1)
- straws (5–10)
- timer (1)

Setup and Instructional Tips

- **Safety Note:** Marbles can be a choking hazard. Remind students to keep them out of their mouths. If this is a concern, ping pong balls can be used instead.
- **Week 1 Day 3:** To save time, set up the ramps for students before the activity, and/or perform one marble race for all students to observe.
- **STEAM Challenge:** This challenge can be done individually or in small groups. If students are working in groups, have students sketch their own designs first. Then, have them compare them in groups and choose one design together.

Discussion Questions

- What is gravity?
- Why doesn't gravity pull us to the center of Earth?
- How are inclined planes used for fun and recreation?
- What happens to an object when it is on a tilted surface?
- In a marble maze, what keeps the marble from rolling to the floor?
- How would our lives be different without gravity?

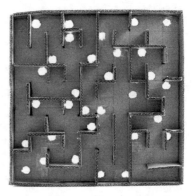

Additional Notes

- **Possible Misconception:** An object at rest, or not moving, has no forces acting on it.
  Truth: An object at rest has balanced forces acting on it—gravity is pulling it down and the solid surface the object is on, such as the ground, is pushing back.

- **Possible Design Solutions:** Students may use straws to make straight walls. They might use pipe cleaners or clay to make curved walls.

Scaffolding and Extension Suggestions

- Support students with timing their mazes by having them practice using a timer beforehand.
- Support students with more maze ideas by helping them look for more examples online.
- Challenge students to add point values to their mazes. Players can try and move marbles to certain areas to gain points in given time limits.

Answer Key

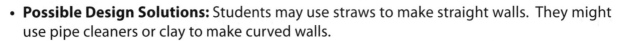

Week 1 Day 1
1. B
2. A
3. D

Week 1 Day 2
1. An inclined plane is a surface that is tilted, such as a ramp.

Week 1 Day 3
1. Marble B should reach the bottom first.
2. Drawings should show a ruler ramp with one end supported by three or more books.

Week 1 Day 5
1. A
2. When the marble hits the side of the track, it stops the marble and pushes it the opposite way.

Weeks 2 & 3
See STEAM Challenge Rubric on page 221.

Day 1

Name: _____ **Date:** _____

Directions: Read the text. Study the diagram. Choose the best answer for each question.

A force is a push or pull. Forces can cause objects to move. Forces can stop objects that are moving. Sometimes, forces can change the directions objects are moving.

Gravity is a force. It pulls objects toward the center of Earth. If you jump in the air, gravity pulls you back to the ground. The ground is solid. It pushes you back. This stops you from falling through it!

downward pull of gravity

upward push of ground

1. Gravity _____.

   (A) pushes you away from Earth

   (B) pulls you toward Earth

   (C) pushes you left

   (D) pulls you right

2. What would happen if you held a ball in the air and let go of it?

   (A) It would fall to the ground.

   (B) It would stay in place.

   (C) It would float up.

   (D) It would spin.

3. Pushes and pulls are types of _____.

   (A) objects

   (B) gravity

   (C) jumps

   (D) forces

Day 2

Name: _____ **Date:** _____

Directions: Read the text. Study the pictures. Answer the questions.

A tilted surface is called an *inclined plane*. Ramps, slides, and hills are all inclined planes. Objects can roll and slide down them. Gravity pulls these objects toward Earth. The solid tilted surfaces push back. This moves the objects down the paths of the inclined planes. Some people go down inclined planes to have fun and go fast.

1. What is an inclined plane?

_____

_____

2. Which picture of an inclined plane looks the most fun? Why?

_____

_____

 Talk About It!

What are some ways you use inclined planes in your daily life?

Name: _____ **Date:** _____

Directions: Set up a marble race. Use the diagrams to help you. Make two ramps that are different heights. Then, release the marbles at the same time. Watch closely to see which marble wins. Repeat the test a few times. Then, answer the questions.

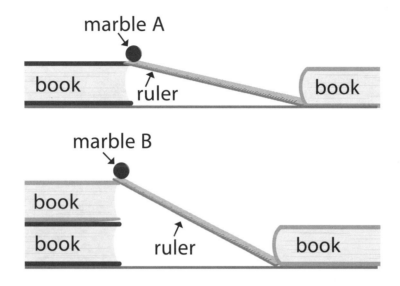

1. Which marble reached the bottom first? _____

2. Imagine there is a third marble to race. You want to make it go even faster. Draw how you would set up the ramp.

Try This!

Make longer ramps. Try putting cardboard tubes together. Race the marbles through the tubes. Does the same marble still win?

Day 4

Name: _____ Date: _____

Directions: Draw a hole for a new miniature golf course. Show it from above. Make a path for the golf ball to roll to reach the hole. Add obstacles in the path. You could add bumps, bridges, or tunnels! Make fun designs, or choose a silly theme.

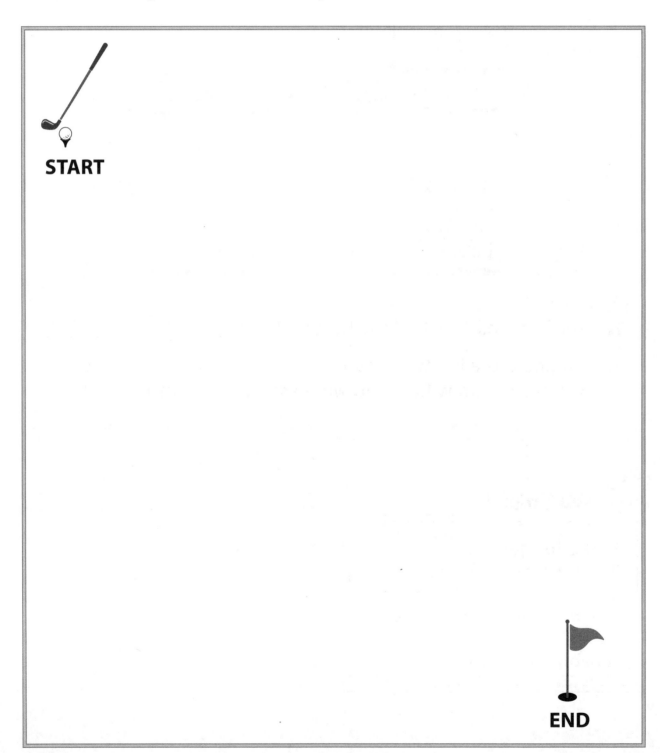

START

END

Name: _____ **Date:** _____

Directions: Read the text. Study the chart. Then, answer the questions.

> A class timed how fast a marble rolled down different tracks. The tracks are made of inclined planes. They recorded the times in the chart.

Track A	Track B	Track C
2 seconds	9 seconds	5 seconds

1. On which track did the marble go the fastest?

   Ⓐ Track A   Ⓒ Track C

   Ⓑ Track B   Ⓓ all of the above

2. Draw on each track. Show the path you think each marble would take. What happens when the marbles hit the sides of the tracks?

_____

_____

_____

Name: _____ Date: _____

Directions: Read the challenge. Then, answer the question.

The Challenge

A toy company has hired you to make a marble maze. People will hold it in their hands to play. People will tilt the maze different ways to move the marble. They will try to move the marble from start to finish.

Criteria

For your marble maze to be successful, it must…

- take a person at least 10 seconds to solve.
- move a marble around by tilting the maze.
- have at least one dead end.
- have a fun theme.

Constraints

- You may only use the materials provided to you.
- Ask your teacher how much time you have. Write it here:

_____

Check for Understanding

1. What questions do you need to ask?

_____

_____

_____

Name: _____ **Date:** _____

Directions: Solve the mazes. Use one color to show the correct path. Use a different color to show paths that lead to dead ends. Then, answer the questions.

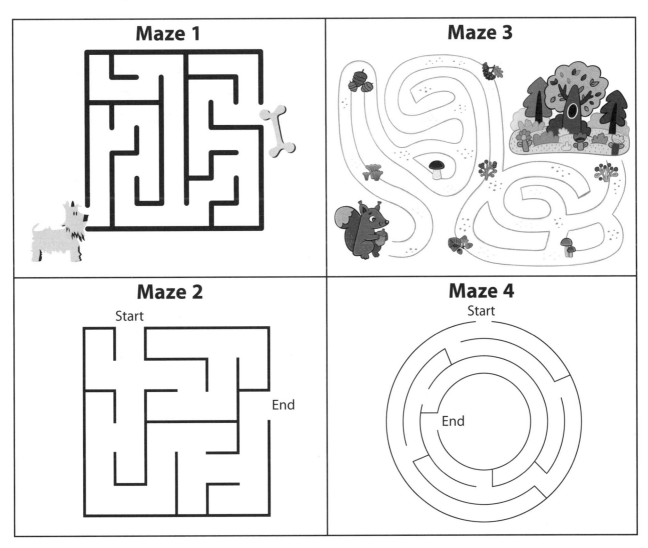

1. Your maze will move a marble as people tilt it. Which materials could you use for the walls in your maze?

   _____

2. What ideas do you have for a theme?

   _____

Unit 1: Fun with Forces

Name: _____ Date: _____

Directions: Sketch your marble maze. Label where it starts and ends. Label the materials for each part.

Quick Tip!

Draw the correct path first. Then, go back and add dead ends and obstacles. Use a pencil so you can erase.

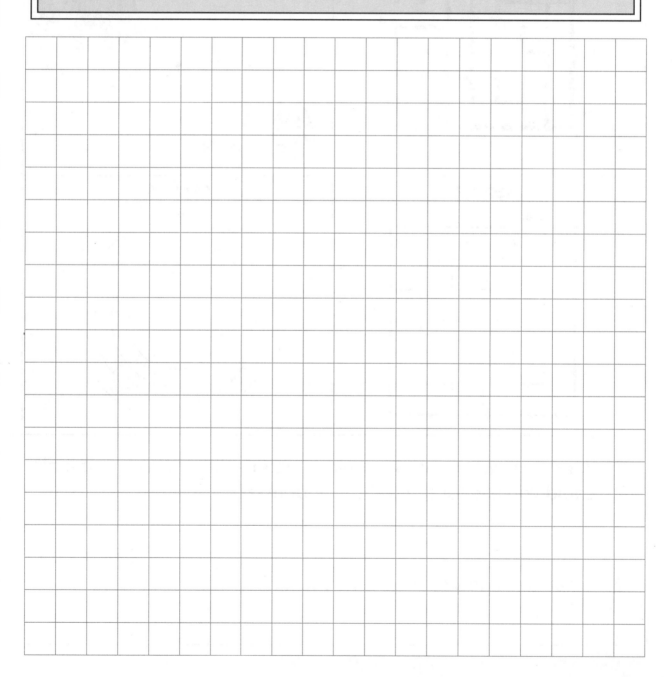

Day 4

Name: _____ **Date:** _____

Directions: Gather your materials. Plan your steps. Build your marble maze. Keep track of problems that come up. Write how you solved them. Then, answer the question.

Steps to Build My Marble Maze

_____   _____

_____   _____

_____   _____

Problems While Building	Solutions

1. Sometimes, engineers change their plans as they build. What changes did you make while building your marble maze?

_____

_____

Name: _____ Date: _____

Directions: Time yourself solving your maze. Time two other people. Record the results. Mark the criteria that were successful.

Tester	Maze Time

My maze…

☐ took at least 10 seconds to solve.

☐ moves a marble around the maze by tilting it.

☐ has at least one dead end.

☐ has a fun theme. The theme is

_____.

Day 1

Name: _____ **Date:** _____

Directions: Think about your marble maze. Answer the questions. Then, plan how you want to improve it.

1. What worked well in your marble maze?

_____

_____

2. What flaws did you find in your marble maze?

_____

_____

Draw a star next to one or more ways you will improve your marble maze.

- My design did not meet the criteria. I will improve it by

_____

_____

- Add more decorations that go with the theme.
- Add more obstacles (dead ends, bumps, tunnels, etc.).
- Add more than one solution to the maze.

- My own idea: _____

_____

Day 2

Name: _____ Date: _____

Directions: Plan your new marble maze design. Then, sketch your new design.

In my redesign, I will…

add _____

remove _____

change _____

Name: _____ **Date:** _____

Directions: Write any new materials you will need. Gather your materials. Plan your steps. Rebuild your marble maze. Record any problems that come up. Write how you solved them.

New Materials

_____   _____

_____   _____

Steps to Rebuild My Marble Maze

_____   _____

_____   _____

_____   _____

Problems While Building	Solutions

Name: _____   **Date:** _____

Directions: Time yourself solving your maze. Time two other people. Record the results. Mark the criteria that were successful. Then, answer the questions.

Tester	Maze Time

My maze…

☐ took at least 10 seconds to solve.

☐ uses gravity to move the marble around the maze.

☐ has at least one dead end.

☐ has a fun theme. It is _____.

1. What criteria did you add to your redesign?

_____

2. Does your new marble maze meet your redesign goals? Write details to explain how you know.

_____

_____

Name: _____ Date: _____

Directions: Think about how you worked on this challenge. Answer the questions.

1. How does gravity help your marble maze work?

    _____

    _____

2. What are you most proud of about this challenge?

    _____

    _____

3. Draw yourself doing something you enjoyed. Write a caption.	4. Draw yourself solving a problem. Write a caption.
      _____ _____	 _____ _____

 Talk About It!

What surprised you about this challenge?

Heating Things Up Teaching Support

Overview of Unit Activities

Students will learn about and explore how heat can cause reversible and irreversible changes through the following activities:

- reading about and studying pictures of how heat changes things
- reading about and studying pictures of changes heat makes to food
- experimenting with heating dried corncobs
- using popcorn to add texture to art
- analyzing a chart showing egg cooking times
- creating popcorn holders

Materials Per Group

Week 1

- colored paper
- dried corn on the cob

- microwaveable popcorn

STEAM Challenge

- basic school supplies
- construction paper

- popcorn (1 microwavable bag's worth; packing peanuts can be substituted)

Setup and Instructional Tips

- **STEAM Challenge:** The challenge can be done individually or in groups. Smaller groups are recommended. Have students sketch their own designs first. Then, have them share designs in groups and choose one together.
- **Testing Days:** Students will need to put popped bags of popcorn in their popcorn holders. Alternatively, they can use 3–4 cups (1 L) of pre-popped popcorn or packing peanuts.

Discussion Questions

- What happens when you add heat to things?
- How do we use heat to improve things?
- What are some changes caused by heat that are reversible?
- What are some changes caused by heat that are not reversible?

Additional Notes

- **Possible Misconception:** Some substances cannot heat up.
  Truth: All substances can heat up, but they go through physical and chemical changes at different temperatures.

- **Possible Design Solutions:** Students may create cone- or cylinder-shaped holders so they can be held and carried easily. Some students may create handles or straps with paper and tape.

Scaffolding and Extension Suggestions

- Challenge students to create popcorn holders that also help insulate popcorn and keep it warm. Additional materials will be necessary.

Answer Key

Week 1 Day 1
1. no
2. B
3. D

Week 1 Day 2
1. A
2. Answers should explain that pasta becomes softer and thicker.

Week 1 Day 5
1. 7–8 minutes
2. That will not fix the problem. Cooking an egg is a change that cannot be undone.

Weeks 2 & 3
See STEAM Challenge Rubric on page 221.

Day 1

Name: _____ Date: _____

Directions: Read the text. Study the diagrams. Choose the best answer for each question.

Everything is made of matter. Matter is anything that takes up space. Matter comes in different forms. It can be solid, liquid, or gas. Adding or removing heat can change matter. Sometimes, these changes are permanent. Sometimes, they are not.

If you put ice in the sun, it will melt. But you can change it back to ice. You just have to put it in a freezer.

If you add too much heat, some things will burn. This change cannot be undone. Wood and paper will turn to ash.

1. Is melting ice a permanent change?   yes   no

2. What happens to wood when it burns?

   (A) It melts.   (C) It turns to rock.

   (B) It turns to ash.   (D) It grows bigger.

3. When water freezes, it changes from a _____.

   (A) solid to a gas   (C) gas to a liquid

   (B) solid to a liquid   (D) liquid to a solid

Day 2

Name: _____ **Date:** _____

Directions: Read the text, and study the pictures. Then, answer the questions.

Heat can change the things we eat. Changes caused by melting or boiling can be undone. Changes caused by cooking or baking cannot be undone.

Before Heat	After Heat
	 Pasta is cooked.
	 An egg is cooked.
	 Butter is melted.
	 Bread is baked.

1. Which change can be reversed, or undone?

   Ⓐ melting butter   Ⓒ cooking an egg

   Ⓑ baking bread   Ⓓ cooking pasta

2. Tell a friend how pasta is different after it is cooked.

Name: _____ Date: _____

Directions: Follow the steps with adult help to see what happens when you heat a whole dried corncob. Answer the questions.

1. Observe the dried corncob closely. Write a prediction. What do you think will happen when the dried corncob is heated?

   _____

   _____

2. Place the corncob in a paper bag. Fold over the top of the bag.

3. Place the paper bag in a microwave. Set the time for 2–3 minutes. Listen closely. What do you hear?

4. Remove the bag from the microwave. Be careful. It might be hot!

5. Open the bag, and look inside. Rip the bag so you can see the whole corncob. Draw and write your observations.

   _____

   _____

   _____

   _____

Talk About It!

Is heating dried corn a change that can be undone? How do you know?

Name: _____ **Date:** _____

Directions: Use popcorn to make art. Draw a picture. Then, add popcorn to it where you like. It will add texture to your art. The popcorn could be leaves on a tree. It could be fur on an animal.

 Try This!

Dip your popcorn in different colors of paint. Then, glue them to your picture. Or, add popcorn seeds to your picture.

Name: _____ Date: _____

Directions: Read the text. Study the chart. Then, answer the questions.

One way to cook eggs is to place them in boiling water. The longer you cook eggs, the harder they get.

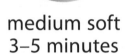

soft-boiled
2–3 minutes

medium soft
3–5 minutes

medium boiled
5–7 minutes

medium hard
7–8 minutes

hard-boiled
8–9 minutes

extra hard
9–10 minutes

1. You want eggs that are medium hard. How long will you leave the eggs in the water?

   _____

2. A recipe says to boil eggs for 3–5 minutes. You leave them for 9 minutes. Your friend tells you to just let them cool down. Will that fix the problem? Explain your answer.

   _____

   _____

   _____

Name: _____ **Date:** _____

Directions: Read the text. Then, answer the question.

The Challenge

It's movie time! People love to eat popcorn while they watch a movie. They also want to reduce waste. So, they want to bring their own popcorn holders. Build a personal popcorn holder.

Criteria

To be successful, your popcorn holder must…

- hold exactly one bag of popped microwaved popcorn. It must all fit. There should not be a lot of extra space.

- be easy to carry with one hand.

Constraints

- You may only use construction paper and tape.

- Ask your teacher how much time you have. Write it here:

_____

Check for Understanding

1. What questions do you need to ask?

_____

_____

_____

_____

Name: _____ Date: _____

Directions: Read the questions. Use them to guide your thinking. Discuss them with others. Record your ideas for your popcorn holder.

What are some shapes of popcorn holders you have seen before?

How big should it be?

Popcorn Holder Brainstorming

How could you make it easy to hold and carry?

What new ideas do you have?

Name: _____ Date: _____

Directions: Sketch two designs for your popcorn holder. Try to make them very different. Draw a star next to your favorite. Or circle your favorite parts of each design. Label the parts.

 Quick Tip!

Think about how you can change the paper to make it work best in your design. Do you need to cut it? Roll it? Fold it?

Design 1	Design 2

Name: _____ **Date:** _____

Directions: Look at your design. Complete the checklist as you prepare and build your popcorn holder. Record notes as you build.

Popcorn Holder Building Checklist

- ☐ Gather materials.
- ☐ Review your design sketch.
- ☐ Write the steps you will follow to build your popcorn holder.

_____   _____

_____   _____

_____   _____

- ☐ Build your popcorn holder.

Building Notes
(challenges, surprises, discoveries, changes, etc.)

Name: _____ Date: _____

Directions: Follow the steps to test your popcorn holder. Answer the questions. Write notes to explain the results. Then, share your popcorn holder with others, and ask for feedback. Write their answers.

1. Pour a bag of popcorn into your holder. Does it all fit without much extra space?

   yes   no

   Notes: _____

   _____

2. Model how to use it. Have one person pick it up with one hand. Can they carry it around easily?

   yes   no

   Notes: _____

   _____

Feedback: Ask and Record

3. What do you like about my popcorn holder?

   _____

   _____

4. If you could change one thing about my design, what would it be?

   _____

   _____

Day 1

Name: _____ Date: _____

Directions: Think about your popcorn holder. Answer the questions. Then, plan how you want to improve it.

1. Did your first design turn out how you hoped? Why or why not?

_____

_____

2. What do you like and want to keep from your first design?

_____

_____

Draw a star next to one or more ways you will improve your popcorn holder.

- My design did not meet the criteria. I will improve it by

_____

_____

- Add a way to carry or hold the popcorn holder without using your hands.
- Make a way for it to be adjustable to fit more or less popcorn.
- Add a part that holds extra melted butter.

- My own idea: _____

_____

Name: _____ **Date:** _____

Directions: Sketch your new popcorn holder design. Complete the sentence.

I think this popcorn holder will work better because _____

_____

_____

Name: _____ **Date:** _____

Directions: Look at your design. Complete the checklist as you prepare and rebuild your popcorn holder. Record notes as you build.

Popcorn Holder Building Checklist

☐ Gather materials.

☐ Review your design sketch.

☐ Write the steps you will follow to build your popcorn holder.

_____ _____

_____ _____

_____ _____

☐ Rebuild your popcorn holder.

Building Notes
(challenges, surprises, discoveries, changes, etc.)

Name: _____ **Date:** _____

Directions: Follow the steps to retest your popcorn holder. Answer the questions as you go. Write notes to explain the results. Then, share your popcorn holder with others. Show them the improvements you made.

1. Pour a bag of popcorn into your holder. Does it all fit without much extra space?

yes   no

Notes: _____

_____

2. Model how to use it. Have one person pick it up with one hand. Can they carry it around easily?

yes   no

Notes: _____

_____

3. Does your new popcorn holder achieve the new goal you set to improve it? Explain your evidence.

_____

_____

4. Does your new popcorn holder work better? Write details to explain how you know.

_____

_____

Name: _____ Date: _____

Directions: Think about how you worked on this challenge. Answer the questions.

1. What did you learn from this challenge?

   _____

   _____

2. What are you most proud of about this challenge?

   _____

   _____

3. Draw yourself doing something you enjoyed. Write a caption.	4. Draw yourself testing your design. Write a caption.
_____ _____	_____ _____

Talk About It!

What surprised you about this challenge?

Materials with Purpose Teaching Support

Overview of Unit Activities

Students will learn about and explore properties of materials and the purposes they serve through the following activities:

- studying words that describe material properties
- reading about and studying pictures of materials used in different clothing
- testing and recording the properties of different objects
- drawing different textures
- analyzing a graph of fabric feature symbols
- creating shoes

Materials Per Group

Week 1

- basic school supplies
- glass jar
- metal coin
- metal spoon

- modeling clay
- plastic bottle
- rubber band
- wooden block

STEAM Challenge

- basic school supplies
- construction paper (3–5 sheets)
- cotton balls (10–20)
- craft foam (3–5 squares)
- craft sticks (10–15)
- felt
- foil

- packing material
- plastic wrap
- rubber bands (5–10)
- rubber erasers (5+)
- sandpaper (2–3 sheets)
- string or ribbon (2 feet, 60 cm)

Setup and Instructional Tips

- **Week 1 Day 3:** Students are asked to test whether materials are waterproof. You may choose to do this part as a group, have them test individually, or record predictions instead of testing that property.
- **STEAM Challenge:** The challenge can be done individually or in groups. If students are working in groups, have students sketch their own designs first. Then, have them share designs in groups and choose one together.

Discussion Questions

- What are some properties of materials?
- Why are material's properties important to engineers?
- How do material's properties affect our choices of materials?
- Are some materials more valuable than others?

Additional Notes

- **Possible Design Solutions:** Students can trace their feet or shoes for sizing. Students might use some absorbent materials on the bottom or soles of their shoes, such as rubber erasers or foam. They might use tougher, stronger materials on the outsides of their shoes. They might use string to make shoelaces.

Scaffolding and Extension Suggestions

- Challenge students to create shoes for a specific purpose, such as playing sports or hiking.

Answer Key

Week 1 Day 1
1. C
2. A
3. D

Week 1 Day 2
Drawings should show a person walking on a cool, windy day with appropriate clothing. They might wear a scarf that is soft or shoes that are tough.

Week 1 Day 5
1. Students may draw images for snow proof or windproof materials.
2. Answers may include: UV protection, heat-resistant, breathable, and stretchy.
3. Fabric symbol should represent a material property not already shown.

Weeks 2 & 3
See STEAM Challenge Rubric on page 221.

Name: _____ Date: _____

Directions: Read the text. Study the chart. Choose the best answer for each question.

All materials have properties. You can use words to describe them. Engineers must know all about the materials they use. They need to know what each material can and cannot do. They must choose materials that are best for each job. The chart shows some words you can use to describe materials.

rough	smooth	absorbent	waterproof
hard	soft	transparent	opaque

1. _____ of materials help engineers know how they can be used.

   (A) Price   (C) Properties

   (B) Names   (D) Locations

2. Which word could describe a material that you can bend?

   (A) flexible   (C) opaque

   (B) firm   (D) waterproof

3. A towel used to soak up water should be _____.

   (A) squishy   (C) hard

   (B) transparent   (D) absorbent

Day 2

Name: _____ Date: _____

Directions: Read the text. Study the pictures. Then, complete the task.

Materials are all around us. Think about the clothes people wear. What they wear depends on what they do and where they go. You might dress one way to play in the snow. You might dress another way to go to sleep.

Some clothes need to be flexible. They let you move easily.

The insides of jackets are often soft. They feel nice.

Backpacks need to be tough so they don't rip.

The bottoms of shoes are elastic and tough. They absorb energy.

1. On another sheet of paper, draw a person walking outside on a cool, windy day. Label the properties of the clothes they might wear. Write as many as you can.

Talk About It!

How would you describe the clothes you are wearing? What properties do the materials have?

Name: _____ Date: _____

Directions: Test and record the properties of different objects. Rate the objects for each property. If you want, choose and test an object of your choice.

	Rating Scale (1–5)					
	1 = Not At All 2 = A Little 3 = Some 4 = Very 5 = Extremely					
	Strong	**Flexible**	**Shiny**	**Waterproof**	**Transparent**	**Smooth**
glass jar						
metal spoon						
plastic bottle						
rubber band						
metal coin						
wooden block						
modeling clay						

Name: _____ **Date:** _____

Directions: You can describe materials by their textures. This is how materials look and feel. Artists have ways to show textures in art. Look at the examples. Try to draw each texture. Then, draw a picture on a separate sheet of paper. Use at least three different textures.

How to Draw Textures	Practice Drawing Textures
rough	
fluffy	
scaly	
furry	
wood grain	

Day 5

Name: _____ **Date:** _____

Directions: Read the text. Study the chart. Then, answer the questions.

Clothes often have tags on them. You might see symbols on these tags. Some of the symbols tell how to care for the material. Some of the symbols tell you the properties of the materials. This can help you choose the clothes you need.

waterproof

stretchy

snowproof

windproof

UV protection

reflective

breathable

lightweight

1. A friend is going on a trip. They think it will snow. They need a new jacket. What symbols should they look for on the clothing tags? Draw one or more.

2. A soccer team needs new uniforms.

What clothing features do you think they should look for?

3. Draw your own clothing symbol. Write what property it represents.

Name: _____ Date: _____

Directions: Read the text. Then, answer the question.

The Challenge

A shoe company has asked you to design a new shoe. They want a shoe that is comfortable. They also want it to protect people's feet and look nice. You will create a single shoe to show for your design.

Criteria

To be successful, your shoe must…

- fit the foot of a person your age.
- be comfortable to wear.
- protect a person's feet when they wear them.
- stay on while walking.

Constraints

- You may only use the materials provided to you.
- Ask your teacher how much time you have. Write it here:

_____

Check for Understanding

1. What questions do you need to ask?

_____

_____

_____

Name: _____ **Date:** _____

Directions: Look in books or online for examples of shoe designs. Choose two examples. Complete the chart.

Shoe Design 1	Shoe Design 2
Sketch	Sketch
What I Like	What I Like
How I Can Use This in My Design?	How I Can Use This in My Design?

Name: _____ Date: _____

Directions: Sketch your shoe design. Label the parts. List the materials you will use. Write one property for each material.

Material	Property

Name: _____ **Date:** _____

Directions: Plan your steps. Gather your materials. Then, build your shoe. Keep notes as you build.

Think About It!

What do you think will be the most challenging part of building your shoe? What can you do to make it easier?

Steps to Build My Shoe

_____   _____

_____   _____

_____   _____

My Building Notes	
Questions	
Challenges	
Changes	

Name: _____ Date: _____

Directions: Put the shoe on one of your feet. Walk around the room with it on. Record the results. Write notes if you need to explain something. Then, ask someone else to try on your shoe. Ask them for warm and cool feedback. Record their ideas.

Criteria	Circle One		Notes
My foot (or another student's) fits in my shoe.	yes	no	
My shoe is comfortable to wear.	yes	no	
My shoe protects a person's foot.	yes	no	
My shoe stays on while walking and feels secure.	yes	no	

Warm Feedback
What do they like?

Cool Feedback
What suggestions do they have?

_____   _____

_____   _____

_____   _____

_____   _____

Name: _____ Date: _____

Directions: Think about your shoe design. Answer the questions. Then, plan how you want to improve it.

1. What worked well in your first shoe design?

    _____

    _____

2. How could you make your shoe more comfortable?

    _____

    _____

   Draw a star next to one or more ways you will improve your shoe design.

   - My design did not meet the criteria. I will improve it by

     _____

     _____

   - Add artistic designs or logos.

   - Add traction to my shoe so it can be worn while hiking.

   - My own idea: _____

     _____

Day 2

Name: _____ Date: _____

Directions: Plan your new shoe design. Then, sketch your new design. Circle any parts or materials that are different or new.

In my redesign, I will…

add _____

remove _____

change _____

Name: _____ Date: _____

Directions: Plan your steps. Gather your materials. Then, rebuild your shoe. Keep notes as you build.

Think About It!

What do you want to do differently during the building process?

Steps to Rebuild My Shoe

_____   _____

_____   _____

_____   _____

My Building Notes	
Surprises	
Challenges	
Changes	

Day 4

Name: _____ Date: _____

Directions: Put the shoe on one of your feet. Walk around the room with it on. Record the results. Write notes to explain or describe the results. Then, answer the questions.

Criteria	Circle One	Notes
My foot (or another student's) fits in my shoe.	yes　　no	
My shoe is comfortable to wear.	yes　　no	
My shoe protects a person's foot.	yes　　no	
My shoe stays on while walking and feels secure.	yes　　no	

1. What criteria did you add to your redesign?

   _____

2. Does your new shoe work better? What is your evidence?

   yes　　　　　no

   _____

   _____

   _____

Day 5

Name: _____ Date: _____

Directions: Think about how you worked on this challenge. Answer the questions.

1. What science concepts were important for this challenge?

   _____

   _____

2. What would you do differently if you did it again?

   _____

   _____

3. What did you enjoy about being a shoe engineer?

   _____

   _____

4. Draw yourself during part of the challenge. Write a caption to tell what you are doing.

   _____

   _____

Talk About It!

What other pieces of clothing or equipment do you want to make next?

Piece by Piece Teaching Support

Overview of Unit Activities

Students will learn about and explore how smaller pieces can be used to create new things through the following activities:

- reading about and studying pictures of how bricks are used to build things
- reading about and studying pictures of how things are put together and taken apart
- building different structures with toy building blocks
- creating art with small pieces of paper
- analyzing a chart of structures students built
- creating model toy structures with specific materials

Materials Per Group

Week 1

- colored paper (cut or torn into scraps)
- toy blocks or sugar cubes (15+)

STEAM Challenge

- basic school supplies
- binder clips (10)
- cardboard tubes (10)
- clothespins (10)
- craft sticks (20)
- pipe cleaners (20)

Setup and Instructional Tips

- **Week 2 Day 1:** Show students the items they will have available to complete the challenge (10 clothespins, 10 binder clips, 20 craft sticks, 20 pipe cleaners, and 10 cardboard tubes)
- **STEAM Challenge:** The challenge can be done individually or in groups. If students are working in groups, have them sketch their own designs first. Then, have them share designs in groups and choose one together.

Discussion Questions

- Why are bricks used for building?
- What are toys or other things you can assemble, disassemble, and reassemble?
- What can be made or built from smaller pieces?
- What types of materials are good for building?
- How are models useful when building?

Additional Notes

- **Possible Design Solutions:** Students may use some or all the materials to create animals, buildings, shapes, or other toys.

Scaffolding and Extension Suggestions

- Discuss how *assemble*, *disassemble*, and *reassemble* are part of the same word family. Discuss the meanings of the prefixes that change the word meanings.
- Challenge students to create multiple model structures with the given materials.
- Challenge students to create model structures with moving parts.

Answer Key

Week 1 Day 1
1. B
2. D
3. C

Week 1 Day 2
1. A
2. Answer should show or describe a structure that can be made with building blocks.

Week 1 Day 5
1. C
2. B
3. Example: Castles are fun to make and not difficult.

Weeks 2 & 3
See STEAM Challenge Rubric on page 221.

Day 1

Name: _____ Date: _____

Directions: Read the text. Study the pictures. Choose the best answer for each question.

Sometimes, objects are put together to make new things. Bricks are one example. Bricks are blocks of dried clay. They are often used to build things. Bricks are strong and can last a long time. Many bricks can be put together to make something bigger. They can be used to make walls, fire pits, and walking paths. Entire buildings can be made of bricks. Kids play with toy bricks.

1. What are bricks?

   Ⓐ blocks of green clay   Ⓒ blocks of wet clay

   Ⓑ blocks of dried clay   Ⓓ blocks of warm clay

2. What can bricks be used to make?

   Ⓐ walls and buildings   Ⓒ walking paths

   Ⓑ fire pits   Ⓓ all of the above

3. Which statement is true?

   Ⓐ Bricks are not good for building.   Ⓒ Bricks are strong.

   Ⓑ Bricks are made of walls.   Ⓓ Only buildings are made of bricks.

Name: _____ Date: _____

Directions: Read the text. Study the pictures. Then, answer the questions.

Many toys are made of pieces. When you put something together, you **assemble** it. The pieces can be put together to make new things. When you're done, you can take the pieces apart, or **disassemble** it. Then, you can **reassemble** the pieces in different ways. You might use all the pieces. Sometimes, you do not need all the pieces to make something new. That is okay! They might be used for something else.

These blocks are assembled as a tower.	Then, they are disassembled into pieces.	The blocks are reassembled into a car.

1. When you put something together for the first time, you _____.

(A) assemble it   (C) reassemble it

(B) disassemble it   (D) unassemble it

2. Draw or describe something else you could make with blocks.

Day 3

Name: _____ Date: _____

Directions: Use small blocks to make different things. Draw what your creations look like in the boxes. Talk about what you learned.

Make a wall.

Make a building.

Make your own idea: _____

Name: _____ **Date:** _____

Directions: Make art with scrap paper. Cut colored paper into small pieces. They can be different shapes and sizes. Use them to make a picture. Move the pieces around on the page. When you like where they are, glue them down. Use markers to add details to your art.

Day 5

Name: _____ Date: _____

Directions: Students in a classroom were given toy blocks. The chart shows what they built. Study the chart. Then, answer the questions.

Structure Built	Number of Students
castle	16
robot	3
cabin	5
animal	5
car	4

1. How many students made cabins or animals?

   Ⓐ 7   Ⓒ 10

   Ⓑ 15   Ⓓ 5

2. What did the fewest number of students make?

   Ⓐ castles   Ⓒ cabins

   Ⓑ robots   Ⓓ cars

3. Look for the structure most students made. Why do you think so many students chose to build that?

   _____

   _____

   _____

   _____

Name: _____ Date: _____

Directions: Read the text. Then, answer the question.

The Challenge

A teacher wants to set up a building center in their classroom. They want to show some fun examples of what kids can build. Your challenge is to create a model structure of what kids can build. It should be interesting and fun for kids to make.

Criteria

To be successful, your model must…

- be assembled, or put together, with some or all the materials.
- be able to be disassembled, or taken apart.
- be a design that is fun and kid-friendly.

Constraints

- You may only use the materials provided to you.
- You may not use tape or glue to keep the materials together.

Check for Understanding

1. Write the challenge in your own words.

_____

_____

Quick Tip!

You can alter two cardboard tubes. Cut them to make smaller pieces. Cut slots on the top and bottom so they fit together.

Name: _____ Date: _____

Directions: Observe the objects you can use for your model structure. Answer the questions in the chart and below it.

Objects	What do you notice? (shape, material, flexible or stiff, etc.)	How could you use these items?
binder clips		
clothespins		
pipe cleaners		
craft sticks		
cardboard tubes		

1. Explore the materials and how they can be put together. Try to make some shapes. Draw what you made.

Name: _____ **Date:** _____

Directions: Sketch two designs for your model structure. Draw a star next to your favorite. Label the parts. Record how many of each material you think you will need.

Design 1	Design 2

Materials	Amount Needed
binder clips	
clothespins	
pipe cleaners	
craft sticks	
cardboard tubes	

Name: _____ Date: _____

Directions: Gather your materials. Plan your steps. Build your model structure. Record any changes you make while building. Tell why you made those changes. Then, answer the question.

My Building Steps

_____   _____

_____   _____

_____   _____

Changes Made While Building	Reason for Changes

What did you build? Describe it. For example, is it a building or an animal? Is it tall or short?

_____

_____

Name: _____ **Date:** _____

Directions: Mark the criteria that were successful. Write notes to explain or describe the results. Then, test if others can make your structure, too.

Criteria	Circle One	Notes
My structure can be assembled with the materials I was given.	yes no	
My structure can be disassembled.	yes no	
My structure is fun and kid-friendly.	yes no	

1. Ask a friend to try to build the structure you made. They can look at yours to help them. Draw what their structure looks like. Write about how close it looks to yours.

_____

_____

Name: _____ Date: _____

Directions: Answer questions to reflect on your model structure. Plan how you can improve it.

1. What do you like best about your structure?

_____

_____

2. What did not work well?

_____

_____

> Draw a star next to one or more ways you will improve your model structure.
>
> • My first structure did not meet all the criteria. In my redesign,
>
>   I will _____
>
>   _____
>
> • Make the design (more/less) challenging for someone else to make.
>
> • My own idea: _____
>
>   _____

Name: _____ Date: _____

Directions: Plan your new design. Then, sketch your new design. Record how many materials you will use.

In my redesign, I will…

add _____

remove _____

change _____

Materials	Amount Needed
binder clips	
clothespins	
pipe cleaners	
craft sticks	
cardboard tubes	

Name: _____ Date: _____

Directions: Gather your materials. Plan your steps. Rebuild your structure. Record the changes you make. Tell why you made those changes.

Think About It!

How do you need to change your steps to rebuild your structure?

Steps to Rebuild

_____   _____

_____   _____

_____   _____

Changes Made While Building	Reason for Changes

Name: _____ **Date:** _____

Directions: Mark the criteria that were successful. Write notes to explain or describe the results. Then, test if others can make your structure, too.

Criteria	Circle One	Notes
My structure can be assembled with the materials I was given.	yes no	
My structure can be disassembled.	yes no	
My structure is fun and kid-friendly.	yes no	

1. Ask the same friend to build the new structure you made. They can look at yours to help them. Draw their structure.

Talk About It!

Ask your friend for feedback. Which structure did they like building more? Why?

Name: _____ Date: _____

Directions: Think about how you worked on this challenge. Answer the questions.

1. What are you most proud of about this challenge?

   _____

   _____

2. What would you do differently next time?

   _____

   _____

3. Kids will be excited to make this structure because

   _____

   _____

   _____

Talk About It!

What was the hardest part of this challenge? How did you overcome it, or persevere?

Biodiversity Teaching Support

Overview of Unit Activities

Students will learn about and explore biodiversity of plants and animals through the following activities:

- reading about and studying images of biodiversity in rainforests
- reading about and studying images of biodiversity in wetlands
- observing biodiversity in different habitats
- drawing aquariums with diverse life and shelter for them all
- analyzing a map of bird diversity in the United States
- creating bird feeders that support observation cameras

Materials Per Group

Week 1

- basic school supplies

STEAM Challenge

- basic school supplies
- birdseed (or something similar)
- clothespins (5–10)
- craft sticks (10–20)
- empty milk/juice carton (1+)
- empty water bottle (1+)
- lime
- paper plates (4–5)
- pipe cleaners (10–20)
- plastic cups (4–5)
- string (2+ feet, 60+ cm)
- toothpicks (10–15)
- wooden skewers (5–10)

Setup and Instructional Tips

- **Week 1 Day 3:** This day requires outdoor access to observe animals and plants. If that is not possible, students can observe animals on live webcams, such as those found at **explore.org**.
- **STEAM Challenge:** The challenge can be done individually or in groups. If students are working in groups, have students sketch their own designs first. Then, have them share their designs in groups and choose one together.
- **Testing Days:** In case of nut allergies, check that the birdseed you get has no nuts.

Discussion Questions

- What is biodiversity?
- Why is biodiversity important?
- What places in the world have the greatest biodiversity? Why?
- How can humans support biodiversity where they live?
- How can observing animals help us protect them?

Additional Notes

- **Possible Misconception:** Biodiversity is the total number of plants and animals.
  Truth: Biodiversity refers to the number of different types of plants and animals.
- **Possible Design Solutions:** Students may try to place the "camera" on top of the birdseed in the center of the bird feeder. Cups, cartons, plates, or bottles can be used to hold birdseed.

Scaffolding and Extension Suggestions

- Have students research the diversity of birds in the areas they live. Encourage them to tailor their bird feeders to meet the needs of specific birds.

Answer Key

Week 1 Day 1
1. B
2. C
3. D

Week 1 Day 2
1. Example: They have fresh water and land. This means many different plants and animals can live there.
2. Example: Wetlands are similar to rainforests because they have tall trees, fresh water, and many different plants and animals.
3. Example: If the water were polluted, the plants and animals in the water would die. Animals that ate plants or animals in the water would die or get sick, too.

Week 1 Day 5
1. Students should draw routes that follow the coastal regions of the United States.
2. Bird diversity might be low in some areas if they do not have fresh water or trees for birds to make nests in.

Weeks 2 & 3
See STEAM Challenge Rubric on page 221.

Name: _____ Date: _____

Directions: Read the text. Choose the best answer for each question.

BIO + DIVERSITY

"life"   "many different types"

Rainforests are home to many types of living things. There are many places for plants and animals to live.

Monkeys and sloths get food and shelter from trees. Birds live in trees, too.

Insects fly around and crawl on the forest floor. Jaguars and tapirs can live on the forest floor.

Rainforests have rivers and streams. Fish, frogs, and alligators can live in or near them. Otters and dolphins can, too.

1. What does *biodiversity* mean?

(A) many types of places   (C) many types of leaves

(B) many types of life   (D) many types of colors

2. Where would you most likely find a sloth?

(A) in a river   (C) in a tree

(B) in a lake   (D) on the forest floor

3. Where would you most likely find a tapir?

(A) in a river   (C) in a tree

(B) in a lake   (D) on the forest floor

Day 2

Name: _____ **Date:** _____

Directions: Read the text. Study the diagram. Answer the questions.

Wetlands are places where the soil is full of water. They are near bodies of fresh water. Swamps, marshes, and bogs are all wetlands. They are home to many different plants and animals.

tall grass

alligator

egret

water lily

muskrat

turtle

fish

1. Why do you think wetlands have so many different animals?

_____

_____

2. How are wetlands similar to rainforests?

_____

_____

3. What might happen if the water was polluted?

_____

_____

Name: _____ **Date:** _____

Directions: Observe the diversity of life near you. Choose two different places, such as a garden, a parking lot, a playground, or a field. Observe each place for at least 5 minutes. Write or draw what you observe. Then, answer the questions.

💡 **Quick Tip!**

Can't find a good place to observe? No problem! Ask an adult to help you find a "critter cam" online. They show live videos of different habitats you can watch.

	Habitat 1	**Habitat 2**
Description of Habitat		
Plants I Saw		
Animals I Saw		
Wildlife I Heard		

1. Where did you see more diversity?

_____

2. Why do you think that is?

_____

_____

Day 4

Name: _____ Date: _____

Directions: Imagine you have a large aquarium. Draw the plants, animals, and decorations you will put in your aquarium.

Name: _____ Date: _____

Directions: This map shows bird species, or types, in the United States. It does not show the total number of birds. It shows where the most variety of birds can be found. Study the map. Then, answer the questions.

Bird Diversity

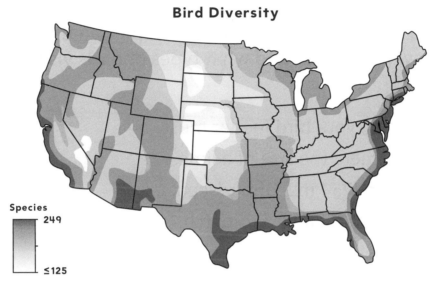

Species
249

≤125

1. Your friend likes to go "birding." They try to find different birds. Plan a road trip for them. Draw the route on the map. Mark where they should start. Circle some places they should stop. Why should your friend follow the route you drew?

_____

_____

_____

2. Look at the areas that have low bird diversity. What do you think might be some reasons for this low level?

_____

_____

Name: _____ Date: _____

Directions: Read the text. Then, answer the questions.

The Challenge

Build a bird feeder that can also hold a small camera. It will record birds when they come to eat. People can use it to keep track of how many birds and what types of birds visit.

Criteria

To be successful, your bird feeder must…

- hold a camera the size of a lime.
- hold 1 cup (250 mL) of birdseed.
- have a place for a bird to perch.

Constraints

- You may only use the materials provided to you.
- Ask your teacher how much time you have. Write it here:

_____

Check for Understanding

1. What are you looking forward to?

_____

_____

2. What do you think will be difficult?

_____

_____

Day 2

Name: _____ Date: _____

Directions: Look in books or online for examples of bird feeders. Choose two examples. They can be homemade or from a store. Sketch them in the chart. Then, answer the questions.

Bird Feeder 1	**Bird Feeder 2**

1. Where are you going to hang your bird feeder?

_____

2. Where could you put the camera? Write or draw your ideas.

Name: _____ Date: _____

Directions: Sketch two designs for your bird feeder. Circle what you like best in each one. Label where the birdseed and camera will go. Label the perch. List the materials.

Design 1	**Design 2**

Materials

_____   _____

_____   _____

_____   _____

Name: _____ Date: _____

Directions: Gather your materials. Plan your steps. Build your bird feeder. Record notes during and after you build.

Steps to Build My Bird Feeder

	Steps	Materials Needed
1		
2		
3		
4		
5		
6		

Building Notes
(challenges, surprises, discoveries, changes, etc.)

Name: _____ Date: _____

Directions: Put the birdseed and the lime in your bird feeder. Hang it up. Record the results. Then, share your bird feeder with others. Ask them for warm and cool feedback. Record their ideas.

Criteria	Circle One	Notes
My bird feeder can hold 1 cup (250 mL) of birdseed.	yes no	
My bird feeder can hold a camera (lime) to record birds.	yes no	
My bird feeder has a place for a bird to perch.	yes no	

Warm Feedback	**Cool Feedback**
What do they like?	What suggestions do they have?

Warm Feedback
What do they like?

_____

_____

_____

_____

Cool Feedback
What suggestions do they have?

_____

_____

_____

_____

Day 1

Name: _____ **Date:** _____

Directions: Think about your bird feeder. Answer the questions. Then, plan how you want to improve it.

1. What do you like most about your bird feeder?

    _____

    _____

2. What did you learn from building and testing your first bird feeder?

    _____

    _____

Draw a star next to one or more ways you will improve your bird feeder.

- My first bird feeder did not meet the criteria. I will try to

    _____

    _____

- Provide more room for birds and birdseed.
- Improve the look of the bird feeder. Add decorations.

- My own idea: _____

    _____

Unit 5: Biodiversity

Name: _____ Date: _____

Directions: Plan how you will change your bird feeder. Sketch your new design. Then, complete the sentence.

Things I Want to Keep	Things I Want to Change

My New Bird Feeder Design

1. I think this design will be better because _____

_____

_____

Name: _____ Date: _____

Directions: Gather your materials. Plan your steps. Rebuild your bird feeder. Record notes as you build.

 Think About It!

> What new materials do you need? How do you need to change your steps?

Steps to Rebuild My Bird Feeder

	Steps	Materials Needed
1		
2		
3		
4		
5		
6		

Building Notes
(challenges, surprises, discoveries, changes, etc.)

Day 4

Name: _____ **Date:** _____

Directions: Retest your bird feeder for all the criteria. Record the results. Then, answer the questions.

Criteria	Circle One	Notes
My bird feeder can hold 1 cup (250 mL) of birdseed.	yes no	
My bird feeder can hold a camera (lime) to record birds.	yes no	
My bird feeder has places for birds to perch.	yes no	

My Redesign Goals

1. In my second design, I wanted to _____

_____

2. Does your new bird feeder meet your redesign goals? Write details to explain how you know.

_____

_____

_____

Name: _____ Date: _____

Directions: Think about how you worked on this challenge. Answer the questions.

1. What science concepts were important for this challenge?

_____

_____

2. What did you enjoy about being an engineer?

_____

_____

3. Draw yourself during part of the challenge. Write a caption to tell what you are doing.

┌───┐
│   │
│   │
│   │
│   │
│   │
│   │
│   │
│   │
│   │
└───┘

Try This!

Try out your bird feeder! Find a place to hang it. Do not worry about the camera. Watch to see if any birds come.

Life Cycle of Frogs Teaching Support

Overview of Unit Activities

Students will learn about and explore the life cycle of frogs through the following activities:

- reading about and studying a diagram of the life cycle of frogs
- reading about and studying pictures of where frogs like to live
- making and playing a matching game about the life cycle of frogs
- creating and drawing frog characters
- analyzing a chart with information about different frog eggs
- creating mini frog habitats

Materials Per Group

Week 1

- basic school supplies

STEAM Challenge

- basic school supplies
- cardboard tubes (2–3)
- modeling clay
- natural materials (grass, sticks, sand, dirt)
- plastic container (to hold frog habitat)
- plastic cups (2)
- rocks of various sizes (3+)
- water (1–3 cups, 250–750 mL)

Setup and Instructional Tips

- **STEAM Challenge:** The challenge can be done individually or in groups. If students are working in groups, have students sketch their own designs first. Then, have them share their designs in groups and choose one together.

Discussion Questions

- What is a life cycle?
- How do human and frog life cycles compare?
- What do frogs need to live and grow throughout all the stages of their lives?
- Why might some frog species be losing their natural habitats?
- How can humans help frogs that live nearby?

Additional Notes

- **Possible Misconception:** Toads are not frogs.
  Truth: This can get complicated, but the short answer is that all toads are frogs. They are part of the same order—Anura. This is similar to how all dolphins are whales, but not all whales are dolphins.

- **Possible Design Solutions:** Students may use cardboard rolls as places for frogs to hide. They should have some water and some areas for frogs to be out of the water, such as on rocks.

Scaffolding and Extension Suggestions

- Have students research frogs that live nearby. Have students design habitats specifically for those species of frogs.

Answer Key

Week 1 Day 1
1. C
2. B
3. A

Week 1 Day 2
1. D
2. There are no frogs in Antarctica because it is so cold, and the only fresh water is ice.

Week 1 Day 5
1. B
2. B
3. All the frogs in the chart lay their eggs in or on fresh water.

Weeks 2 & 3
See STEAM Challenge Rubric on page 221.

Unit 6: Life Cycle of Frogs

Day 1

Name: _____ **Date:** _____

Directions: Read the text. Study the diagram. Choose the best answer for each question.

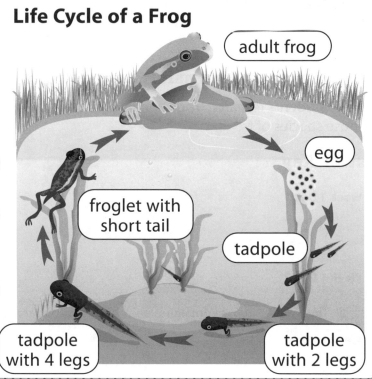

Life Cycle of a Frog

Frogs are amphibians. They live some of their lives in the water and some on land. When they are young, they have gills and tails. These help them live in the water. As they grow, their bodies change. An adult frog has lungs and legs. These help them live on land.

adult frog

egg

froglet with short tail

tadpole

tadpole with 4 legs

tadpole with 2 legs

1. Where do frogs live?

　Ⓐ　only in water　　　Ⓒ　in water and on land

　Ⓑ　only on land

2. What stage comes just before the froglet stage?

　Ⓐ　tadpole with two legs and a long tail

　Ⓒ　tadpole with four legs and no tail

　Ⓑ　tadpole with four legs and a long tail

　Ⓓ　tadpole with two legs and a short tail

3. Which body parts help frogs live on land?

　Ⓐ　lungs and legs　　　Ⓒ　gills and a tail

　Ⓑ　a tail and legs　　　Ⓓ　gills and lungs

Day 2

Name: _____ **Date:** _____

Directions: Read the text. Study the pictures. Then, answer the questions.

Frogs live all over the world. Antarctica is the only continent where frogs do not live.

Adult frogs use their lungs to breathe. They also breathe through their skin. Frogs drink water through their skin, too. Most frogs need their skin to stay moist. So, they make their homes near fresh water. They like ponds, lakes, and streams.

Some frogs live in trees. They get water from the air. In dry places, frogs can dig holes in the ground to find water. If it gets too cold or too hot, frogs will hide in holes or under leaves. Good hiding places also keep frogs safe from predators.

A frog hides in a pipe.

A frog sits in a hole.

1. Frogs use their skin to _____.

   Ⓐ drink and eat   Ⓒ eat and dig

   Ⓑ breathe and smell   Ⓓ drink and breathe

2. Why do you think there are no frogs in Antarctica?

   _____

   _____

Name: _____ **Date:** _____

Directions: Draw each stage of the frog life cycle. Explain to a friend how a frog changes.

egg	tadpole
tadpole with 2 legs	tadpole with 4 legs
froglet with short tail	adult frog

Name: _____ **Date:** _____

Directions: Read the text. Complete the task.

There is just something special about frogs. They are used in many types of art. There are famous frog characters in books, fairy tales, movies, and shows. Can you name any?

Task: Make your own frog character! Write details about your frog character. Then, draw and color your frog character.

Character Name	
Character Traits (funny, smart, clumsy, etc.)	
Abilities (speaks, jumps high, plays soccer, etc.)	
Accessories (hat, sunglasses, etc.)	

Try This!

Write a story. Make your frog the main character!

Name: _____ **Date:** _____

Directions: Frogs lay their eggs at specific times and in specific places. Study the chart. Then, answer the questions.

Species	When It Lays Eggs	Location of Eggs	Time Before Hatching
Western Chorus Frog	March–April	in water, wrapped around grass or twigs	6–18 days
Northern Leopard Frog	April	in water, on plants	13–20 days
Green Frog	May–July	floating on the surface of water	3–5 days

1. A tadpole hatches in under a week. Which species of frog could it be?

   (A) Western Chorus Frog

   (B) Western Chorus Frog or Green Frog

   (C) Green Frog or Northern Leopard Frog

   (D) Northern Leopard Frog

2. None of these frogs lay eggs in _____.

   (A) summer

   (B) fall or winter

   (C) winter or spring

   (D) spring

3. What is similar about where these frogs lay their eggs?

_____

_____

Name: _____ Date: _____

Directions: Read the text. Then, answer the question.

The Challenge

Frogs can be helpful to have in your garden. They eat insects that like to eat plants. Create a model of a frog habitat for a garden or yard.

Criteria

To be successful, your frog habitat must…

- support all stages of a frog's life cycle.
- provide at least two places for frogs to hide.

Constraints

- You may only use the materials provided to you.
- Ask your teacher how much time you have. Write it here:

_____

Check for Understanding

1. What questions do you need to ask?

_____

_____

_____

_____

Name: _____ **Date:** _____

Directions: Think about what you have learned about frogs. Answer the questions. Then, write any other research questions you have. Search for answers in books or online. Write the answers you find.

1. How could your habitat support frog eggs?

   _____

   _____

2. How could your habitat support tadpoles?

   _____

   _____

3. How could your habitat support adult frogs?

   _____

   _____

Other Questions I Want to Research	Answers

Name: _____ **Date:** _____

Directions: Sketch your frog habitat design. Label the parts and materials. Draw frog eggs, tadpoles, and at least one adult frog. Show where each would live. Then, complete the sentence.

1. My design will attract frogs because _____

_____

Name: _____ Date: _____

Directions: Gather your materials. Plan your steps. Build your frog habitat. Then, answer the question.

Talk About It!

What do you think will be difficult?
How could you make it easier?

Steps to Build My Frog Habitat

_____   _____

_____   _____

_____   _____

1. Compare your design to what you built. How are they different?

_____

_____

_____

Quick Tip!

If a material is not working how you want, try a different option.

Name: _____ Date: _____

Directions: Answer the questions to assess your frog habitat. Share your frog habitat with others. Tell them about each part. Discuss whether they agree with your answers.

1. Does your habitat have a place for eggs to float or attach?

   yes   no

   Explain: _____

   _____

2. Does your habitat have a place for tadpoles to swim?

   yes   no

   Explain: _____

   _____

3. Will frogs be able to get out of the water and sit?

   yes   no

   Explain: _____

   _____

4. Does your habitat have at least two places for frogs to hide?

   yes   no

   Explain: _____

   _____

Day 1

Name: _____ Date: _____

Directions: Think about your frog habitat. Answer the questions. Then, plan how you want to improve it.

1. What do you think frogs would like best about your frog habitat?

_____

_____

2. What changes do you need to make to meet the criteria?

_____

_____

3. What materials do you need to change or get more of?

_____

_____

Draw a star next to one or more ways you will improve your frog habitat.

- My first design did not meet the challenge criteria. I will make changes so it does.
- Provide more shelter or places to hide.
- Add decorations so people will want to put it in their gardens.
- Write directions. This will help people make their own.

- My own idea: _____

_____

Name: _____ **Date:** _____

Directions: Plan your new frog habitat. Sketch your new design.
Circle any parts or materials that are different or new. Then, complete
the sentence.

In my redesign, I will…

add _____

remove _____

change _____

[ ]

1. I think this design will work better because _____

_____

Name: _____ Date: _____

Directions: Write any new materials you will need. Gather your materials. Plan your steps. Rebuild your frog habitat. Write notes about the building process.

New Materials

_____   _____

_____   _____

Think About It!

What do you need or want to do differently as you rebuild?

Steps to Rebuild My Frog Habitat

_____   _____

_____   _____

_____   _____

Building Notes
(problems, questions, changes)

Name: _____ **Date:** _____

Directions: Put a check next to each statement that is true. Answer the questions. Share your new design with others. Discuss whether they agree with your answers.

> ❑ My frog habitat has a place for eggs to float or attach.
>
> ❑ My frog habitat has a place for tadpoles to swim.
>
> ❑ My frog habitat has places for frogs to get out of the water and rest.
>
> ❑ My frog habitat has two or more places for frogs to hide.

1. In my redesign, I wanted to _____

_____

2. Does your new frog habitat meet your redesign goals? Write details to explain how you know.

_____

_____

_____

_____

Name: _____ **Date:** _____

Directions: Think about how you worked on this challenge. Answer the questions.

1. What science concepts did you need to know for this challenge?

   _____

   _____

2. What are you most proud of about this challenge?

   _____

   _____

3. Draw something you enjoyed. Write a caption.	4. Draw something that was hard. Write a caption.
_____ _____	_____ _____

Talk About It!

What other animals could you create homes for? What would the homes look like?

Plant Survival Teaching Support

Overview of Unit Activities

Students will learn about and explore what plants need and how they survive through the following activities:

- reading about and studying a diagram of parts of plants and what they do
- reading about and studying pictures of plants that have special adaptations
- investigating whether carrot tops regrow better with sunlight
- drawing dream gardens
- analyzing a plant care guide
- creating a watering can

Materials Per Group

Week 1

- carrot tops [2; about 1 inch (2.5 cm) long]
- clear cups or jars (2)
- dark area, such as a cabinet

- sunny area by a window
- toothpicks (8)
- water (1–2 cups, 250–500 mL)

STEAM Challenge

- basic school supplies
- cardboard tubes (3–5)
- craft sticks (5–10)
- duct tape (optional)
- foil
- hole puncher or push pins (optional; for making holes in materials)
- measuring cup
- plastic wrap

- recycled containers with lids (2+; coffee cans, milk cartons, plastic jugs, water bottles)
- straws (5+)
- string (2–3 feet, 1 m)
- various decorating materials (beads, ribbon, paint, etc.)
- water (3 cups, 750 mL)

Setup and Instructional Tips

- **Week 1 Day 3:** Students will need to observe the carrots over several days to see new growth. If carrots are not available, this can also be done with garlic cloves, green onions, or sweet potatoes.

- **STEAM Challenge:** The challenge can be done individually or in groups. If students are working in groups, have students sketch their own designs first. Then, have them share their designs in groups and choose one together.

- **Building Days:** Adults should make holes in students' materials, as needed.

- **Safety Note:** When students test watering cans, be cautious of floor surfaces that become slippery when wet.

Discussion Questions

- What do plants need to live and grow?
- How do plants get what they need?
- Why are plants important to people?
- How can people help plants live and grow?
- What plants do you think are the most interesting?

Additional Notes

- **Possible Misconception:** Plants are not alive.
  Truth: Plants are living things, even though they are very different from animals.
- **Possible Misconception:** Trees are not plants.
  Truth: Trees are types of plants with trunks (stems) and branches.
- **Possible Design Solutions:** The main part of the watering cans should be made from one or more waterproof containers (e.g., plastic). Students might use straws to create and extend the spouts of their watering cans. Students might create handles with string, cardboard, or craft sticks.

Scaffolding and Extension Suggestions

- Support students, if needed, by providing them with plastic milk or detergent jugs to start with. They can adjust this predesigned frame for their watering cans.
- Challenge students to create watering cans for high-hanging plants, for which they will need to consider how to pour or push the water when it is up high.
- Read and discuss the book, *Living Sunlight: How Plants Bring the Earth to Life* by Sallie W. Chisholm.

Answer Key

Week 1 Day 1
1. D
2. A
3. B

Week 1 Day 2
1. The house plant grows like that to get sunlight.
2. Kelp grows from the bottom of the ocean. To reach the sunlight, it must grow fast and tall.
3. The roots of a desert plant help it get as much water as it can when it rains.

Week 1 Day 5
1. B
2. C
3. Example: I would tell my friend to get aloe vera. It does not need much sunlight. It only needs water every 2 weeks.

Weeks 2 & 3
See STEAM Challenge Rubric on page 221.

Name: _____ **Date:** _____

Directions: Read the text. Study the diagram. Choose the best answer for each question.

Plants are living things. They need sunlight and water to live, grow, and reproduce. They need sunlight and water to make their food. Plants have special parts that help them get what they need. Roots absorb water. Leaves absorb sunlight. Stems hold plants up and move their leaves toward the sun. Stems also help transport water from the roots to the rest of the plants.

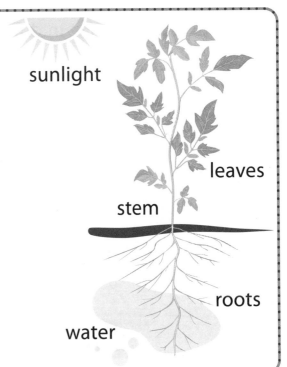

1. Why do plants need sunlight and water?

   Ⓐ to live and grow

   Ⓑ to reproduce

   Ⓒ to make food

   Ⓓ all of the above

2. How do roots help a plant live?

   Ⓐ They absorb water.

   Ⓑ They absorb sunlight.

   Ⓒ They hold the plant up.

   Ⓓ They make the plant's food.

3. What plant part helps absorb sunlight?

   Ⓐ stem

   Ⓑ leaves

   Ⓒ roots

   Ⓓ soil

Name: _____   Date: _____

Directions: Read the text. Study the pictures. Then, answer the questions.

Plants grow and live in different places. Their roots, stems, and leaves work in special ways to get sunlight and water.

Some house plants grow toward sunlight.

Desert plants have complex root systems.

Giant kelp grows in the ocean. It must grow very fast and very tall.

1. Why do you think the house plant grows like that?

_____

2. Why do you think kelp must grow fast and tall?

_____

3. How might more roots help a desert plant get what it needs?

_____

_____

Name: _____ **Date:** _____

Directions: Read the text, and study the diagram. Follow the steps.

> A carrot is a special type of root. Try growing plants from carrot tops. Test different sunlight conditions.
>
> **Materials:** 2 carrot tops, 2 clear cups, toothpicks, water

Step 1: Label your cups.

- Cup A: Water and Sun
- Cup B: Water, No Sun

Step 2: Prepare each carrot top as shown.

Step 3: Place Cup A near a window. Place Cup B in a dark place.

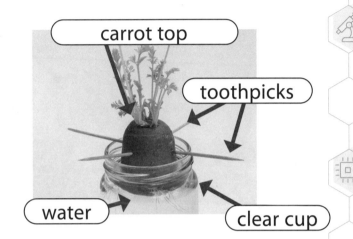

Step 4: Check your carrots every day for 5 days. Add water as needed. Discuss any changes you notice.

Step 5: After 5 days, draw the results. Discuss the results with others.

Observations After Five Days	
Cup A: Water and Sun	Cup B: Water, No Sun

Name: _____ Date: _____

Directions: Draw your very own dream garden. Add as many plants as you want. They can be real or pretend. They can be any size, shape, or color you want. Draw yourself sitting on a bench in your garden.

Name: _____ Date: _____

Directions: Different plants need different amounts of sunlight and water. Study the chart. Then, answer the questions.

Plant Care Guide

Types of Plants	Aloe Vera	Mint	Peace Lily	Sunflower
Amount of Sunlight	low to medium (3–6 hours)	medium to full (4–8 hours)	low (3–4 hours)	full (6–8 hours)
How Often to Water	every 2 weeks	every 2 days	twice a week	once a week

1. Which plant needs water the most often?

   Ⓐ aloe vera   Ⓒ peace lily

   Ⓑ mint   Ⓓ sunflower

2. Which place would be the best spot to grow sunflowers?

   Ⓐ inside, away from the window   Ⓒ outside in an open field

   Ⓑ inside, near the window   Ⓓ in a garden, under a tree

3. Your friend wants an indoor plant that is easy to care for. Which plant would you suggest? Why?

   _____

   _____

Name: _____ Date: _____

Directions: Read the text. Then, answer the question.

The Challenge

A new garden store is opening near you. You have been asked to design a new watering can to be sold there. It will help people water their plants.

Criteria

To be successful, your watering can must…

- hold at least 3 cups (750 mL) of water.
- be easy for someone to carry and pour with one hand.
- pour water gently, not all at once.

Constraints

- You may only use the materials provided to you.
- Ask your teacher how much time you have. Write it here:

_____

Check for Understanding

1. Write the challenge in your own words.

_____

_____

_____

_____

Name: _____ **Date:** _____

Directions: Find examples of different watering cans. Write or draw ideas you like in the chart. Add your own ideas. Discuss your ideas with others.

Materials	Shapes

How the Water Pours	Unique or Fun Ideas

Name: _____ Date: _____

Directions: Sketch your watering can. Draw two or three options. Try to sketch designs that use different materials. Draw a star next to your favorite. Label the parts. List the materials you will use.

Materials

_____   _____

_____   _____

_____

Name: _____ **Date:** _____

Directions: Look at your design. Complete the checklist as you prepare and build your watering can. Then, answer the question.

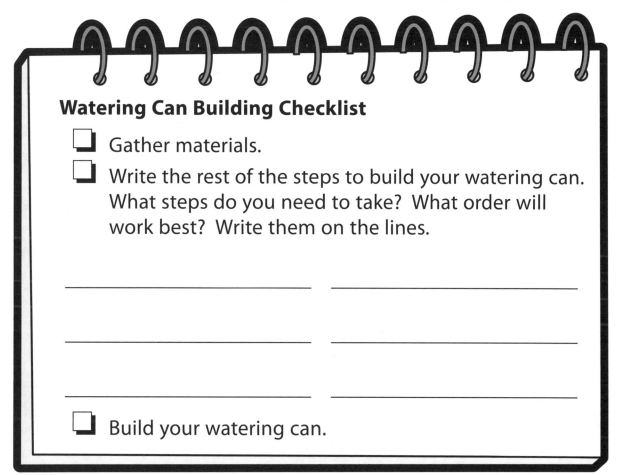

Watering Can Building Checklist

❑ Gather materials.

❑ Write the rest of the steps to build your watering can. What steps do you need to take? What order will work best? Write them on the lines.

_____   _____

_____   _____

_____   _____

❑ Build your watering can.

1. Did you make any design changes as you were building? Write or draw them here.

Day 5

Name: _____ Date: _____

Directions: Follow the steps to test your watering can. Answer the questions. Write notes to explain the results.

1. Pour 3 cups (750 mL) of water into your watering can. Does the water fit and stay in the can?

yes   no

Notes: _____

_____

2. Model how to use it. Pick it up with one hand. Can you carry it?

yes   no

Notes: _____

_____

3. Model how to water a plant with it. Pour some water into an empty container. Did it pour slowly?

yes   no

Notes: _____

_____

4. Watch closely as others test their watering cans. What did you notice or learn?

_____

_____

Day 1

Name: _____ **Date:** _____

Directions: Think about your watering can. Answer the questions. Then, plan how you want to improve it.

1. What worked well in your watering can design?

_____

_____

2. What could make your watering can work better?

_____

_____

3. How could the redesign changes help your design?

_____

_____

    You will have the chance to redesign your watering can. You have a new creative goal. It must have visual appeal. The way it looks should make customers want to buy it. Write or draw as many ideas as you can.

Name: _____ Date: _____

Directions: Sketch two new designs. Draw a star next to your favorite. Answer the questions about your choice.

Redesign 1	**Redesign 2**

1. Why do you think the design you chose will work better?

   _____

   _____

2. Why will customers want to buy it?

   _____

   _____

Name: _____ **Date:** _____

Directions: Look at your design. Complete the checklist. Then, rebuild your watering can. Answer the question.

Think About It!

What did you learn from your first attempt? What should you do differently this time?

Steps to Rebuild My Watering Can

☐ Gather materials.

☐ Write the rest of the steps to rebuild your watering can.

_____   _____

_____   _____

_____   _____

1. Did you make any design changes as you were building? Write or draw them here.

Name: _____ **Date:** _____

Directions: Follow the steps to test your new design. Record the results. Use words and drawings to tell what happened. Then, answer the questions.

Steps

1. Pour 3 cups (750 mL) of water in your watering can.

2. Model how to carry it.

3. Model how to water a plant with it. If you want, try watering a real plant this time!

Results

---

1. Did your new watering can design work better? Explain why or why not.

_____

_____

2. How did you add visual appeal?

_____

_____

Name: _____ **Date:**_____

Directions: Present your design to others. Share how it works. Explain the visual appeal. Ask for feedback. Then, answer the questions.

Visual Appeal Feedback

1. What do others like about the look of your watering can?

_____

2. What suggestions do others have about the look of your watering can?

_____

_____

Reflections

3. What did you enjoy about this challenge?

_____

_____

4. What would you do differently next time?

_____

_____

Talk About It!

What did you learn or achieve from redesigning your watering can?

Pollination Partners Teaching Support

Overview of Unit Activities

Students will learn about and explore how animals support the pollination process through the following activities:

- reading about and studying a diagram of the parts of a flower
- reading about and studying images of animal pollinators
- experimenting with using fingers as pollinators
- creating bright-colored coffee-filter flowers
- analyzing a chart of pollinator preferences
- creating hand pollinators

Materials Per Group

Week 1

- basic school supplies
- cheese puffs (3–5)
- circular coffee filter
- zip-top bag

STEAM Challenge

- basic school supplies
- clothespins (2–3)
- colored chalk powder
- cotton balls (3–5)
- cotton swabs (3–5)
- craft puff balls (5+)
- craft sticks (5–10)
- double-sided tape
- paper baking cups (4)
- pipe cleaners (3–5)
- wooden skewers (5)
- yarn

Setup and Instructional Tips

- **Week 1 Day 3:** Prepare for this activity by placing a few cheese puffs in a zip-top bag for each student. If there is an issue using cheese puffs due to allergies, glitter or juice powder can be substituted. Students can save their "pollen" by covering it with tape on their activity sheets.

- **STEAM Challenge:** The challenge can be done individually or in groups. If students are working in groups, have students sketch their own designs first. Then, have them share their designs in groups and choose one together.

Discussion Questions

- What is pollination?
- What are the different parts of a flower?
- How are flowers similar to and different from each other?
- Why are animal pollinators important?
- How can people help pollinate plants?

Additional Notes

- **Possible Misconception:** All plants have flowers.
  Truth: Only some plants have flowers and grow fruit.

- **Possible Design Solutions:** Students may place cotton balls on the ends of their hand pollinators to pick up the "pollen." They might add a shaking movement to their pollinators to help release the pollen.

Scaffolding and Extension Suggestions

- Help students search online for examples of hand pollinators others have made.
- Challenge students to reach pollen that is not as easy to access. For example, place the pollen inside a long cardboard tube.

Answer Key

Week 1 Day 1
  1. A
  2. B
  3. C

Week 1 Day 2
  1. The beak of a hummingbird is skinny and long. It can reach into the center of a flower to get nectar.
  2. If there were no more bumblebees, tomato plants might not make many seeds. They would not grow many new plants.

Week 1 Day 3
  1. D
  2. The cheese powder came off more when rubbing fingers together.

Week 1 Day 5
  1. Bats would like the Saguaro flower because it opens at night. It also smells fruity and moldy.
  2. Bees like sunflowers because they are yellow and smell sweet. Sunflowers are also large and flat.

Weeks 2 & 3
See STEAM Challenge Rubric on page 221.

Name: _____ Date: _____

Directions: Read the text. Study the diagram. Then, answer the questions.

Some plants have flowers. Flowers make seeds. The parts of a flower help make seeds. The seeds can grow into new plants.

Flowers need pollen to make seeds. Pollen looks and feels like powder. It is often yellow or some other bright color. It is what makes some people sneeze. The anthers make and hold a flower's pollen. The stigma is sticky. It traps and holds pollen. Petals protect the center of a flower. They also give animal pollinators places to land. Pollinators help move pollen from flower to flower.

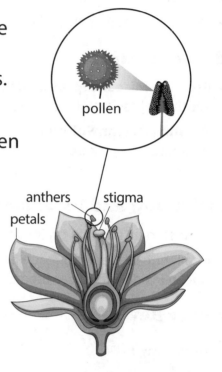

1. Why do flowers need pollen?

   Ⓐ to make seeds   Ⓒ to grow more leaves

   Ⓑ to make nectar   Ⓓ to grow petals

2. Why would it be helpful for the stigma to be sticky?

   Ⓐ so insects will get stuck   Ⓒ to protect the flower from animals

   Ⓑ so pollen will stick   Ⓓ to absorb sunlight

3. Where is a flower's pollen located?

   Ⓐ around the outside   Ⓒ on top of the anthers

   Ⓑ near the leaves   Ⓓ at the bottom of the stigma

Name: _____ **Date:** _____

Directions: Read the text. Study the pictures. Then, answer the questions.

Animal pollinators help spread pollen from flower to flower. Hummingbirds are pollinators. So are butterflies. They get nectar from flowers. Nectar is a sweet liquid. It is in the center of flowers. Hummingbirds get pollen on their beaks. Butterflies get pollen on their wings.

Bees get nectar and pollen from flowers. Bumblebees have a unique way to get pollen that is hard to reach. It is called *buzz pollination*. A bumblebee lands on a flower and grabs the anthers. It buzzes very loud. This vibrates the flower. It shakes the pollen loose. The bee keeps some of the pollen for food. Pollen also sticks to its body.

1. How does the shape of a hummingbird's beak help it get nectar?

_____

2. Tomato plants need buzz pollination to make seeds. What might happen to tomato plants if there were no more bumblebees?

_____

_____

Day 3

Name: _____ Date: _____

Directions: Would your fingers make good pollinators? Follow the steps to find out. Then, answer the questions.

1. Open a bag of cheese puffs. Put your thumb and pointer finger in the bag. Move them around.

2. Place the same fingers in the center of the flower. Press down a few times. Try rubbing your fingers together.

Target

1. What does the cheese powder represent in this activity?

   Ⓐ petals   Ⓒ nectar

   Ⓑ bees   Ⓓ pollen

2. What happened when you rubbed your fingers together?

   _____

   _____

© Shell Education

Name: _____ Date: _____

Directions: Most pollinators are attracted to bright colors. Make a colorful flower of your own. Plan a colorful design in the circle. Then, use markers to draw your design on a coffee filter. Spray water on your design. Watch what happens.

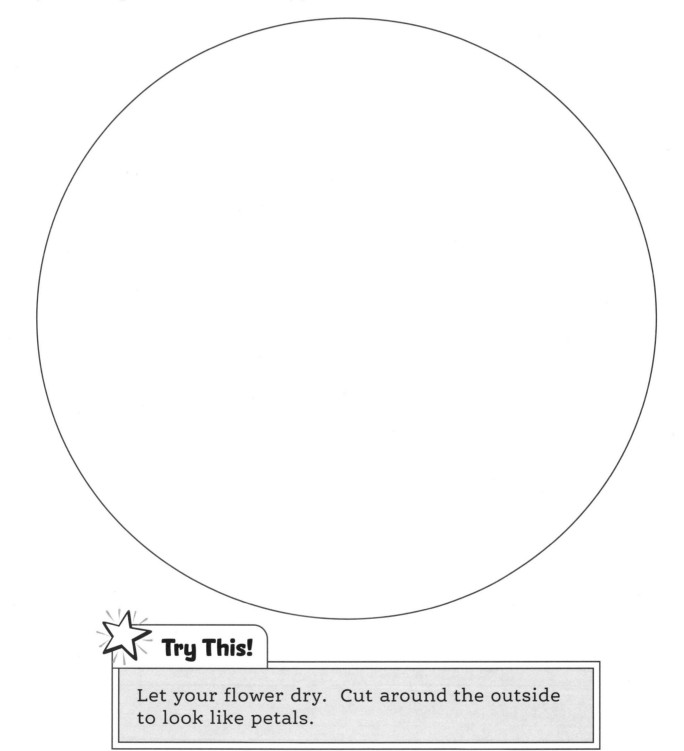

Try This!

Let your flower dry. Cut around the outside to look like petals.

Name: _____ Date: _____

Directions: The chart shows what different pollinators prefer. Study the chart. Then, answer the questions.

Pollinator Preferences

Pollinators	bats 	bees 	birds 	butterflies 
Color	dull white, green, and purple	bright white, yellow, blue	red, orange, or white	red, purple, and other bright colors
Odor	strong; damp, moldy, fruity; smells at night	fresh, mild, sweet, minty	none	faint but fresh
Shape	regular; bowl-shaped; closed during the day	shallow or flat; large place to land; tube-shaped	large; funnel-shaped; cup-shaped	narrow tube; groups of small flowers

1. The Saguaro flower opens at night. It can smell like overripe fruit. Which pollinator do you think would like it? Why?

   _____

   _____

2. Why might bees like sunflowers?

   _____

   _____

Name: _____ Date: _____

Directions: Read the text. Then, answer the question.

The Challenge

The number of bees in the world has gone down. Farmers need help. Design a pollinator that can be used by hand. It should be able to pollinate flowers from a distance. Your goal is to transfer as much pollen as you can.

Criteria

To be successful, your hand pollinator must…

- transfer pollen (chalk powder) from one flower (paper baking cup) to another.
- allow a user to reach flowers from 3 feet (1 m) away.

Constraints

- You may only use the materials provided to you.
- Ask your teacher how much time you have. Write it here:

_____

Check for Understanding

1. What questions do you need to ask?

_____

_____

_____

_____

Name: _____ **Date:** _____

Directions: Think about what you know about pollination. Read the questions. Use them to guide your thinking. Then, brainstorm some ideas for a design. Record your ideas. Share your ideas with others.

What ideas can you use from real pollinators?

How will the pollen stick?

What new ideas do you have?

What questions do you have?

What materials will work best?

Hand Pollinator Ideas

Name: _____ Date: _____

Directions: Sketch two designs for your hand pollinator. Draw a star next to your favorite. Or, circle your favorite parts of each design. Label the parts. Then, answer the questions.

Design 1	Design 2

1. How will your design collect pollen from the flowers?

_____

_____

2. How will your design leave or release pollen on other flowers?

_____

_____

Day 4

Name: _____ Date: _____

Directions: Plan your steps. Gather your materials. Then, build your hand pollinator. Keep notes as you build. Then, answer the question.

Steps to Build My Hand Pollinator

_____ _____

_____ _____

_____ _____

My Building Notes	
Questions	
Challenges	
Changes	

1. What do you think will happen when you test your device?

_____

_____

Name: _____ Date: _____

Directions: Study the diagram. Use it to set up your test. Stand next to Cup A. Then, test how much pollen you can transfer from Cup A to Cup B. Record the results. Answer the questions.

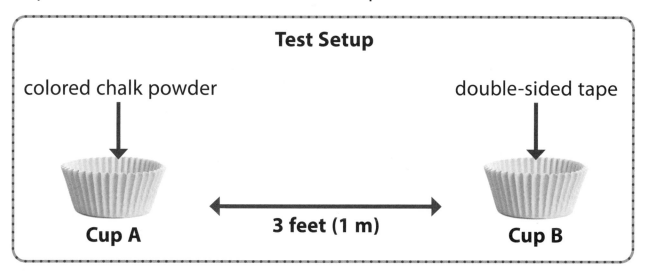

Test Setup

colored chalk powder   double-sided tape

Cup A ←—— 3 feet (1 m) ——→ Cup B

Results

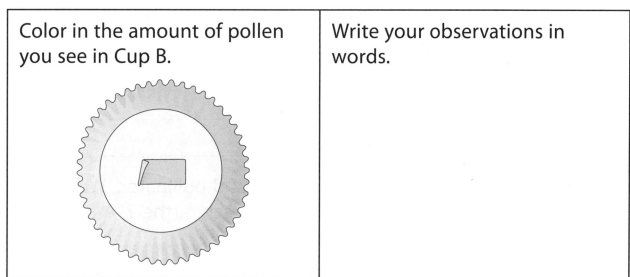

Color in the amount of pollen you see in Cup B.	Write your observations in words.

1. Could your hand pollinator reach 3 feet (1 m)?   yes   no

2. Did your hand pollinator meet the goals of the challenge? Explain why or why not.

_____

_____

Day 1

Name: _____ Date: _____

Directions: Think about your hand pollinator design. Answer the questions. Then, plan how you want to improve it.

1. What worked well with your hand pollinator design?

   _____

   _____

2. What about your design could work better?

   _____

   _____

3. What was hard about making and testing your first design?

   _____

   _____

Write how you want to improve your hand pollinator. Write a goal. Will it transfer more pollen? Will it reach farther? Are there other ways it could be more useful?

Goal: My new design will _____

_____

_____

_____

Name: _____ Date: _____

Directions: Plan your new hand pollinator design. Then, sketch your new design. Circle any parts or materials that are different or new. Write the materials needed.

1. Do you want to change or add materials?   yes   no

2. Do you want to change the shape of your hand pollinator?

   yes   no

My Hand Pollinator Redesign

Materials

_____   _____

_____   _____

Name: _____ **Date:** _____

Directions: Plan your steps to rebuild. Gather your materials. Then, rebuild or adjust your hand pollinator. Keep notes as you build. Answer the question.

Steps to Rebuild My Hand Pollinator

_____ _____

_____ _____

_____ _____

My Building Notes	
Challenges	
Questions	
Changes	

1. How confident are you with your new hand pollinator? Circle one. Explain your choice.

very confident   somewhat confident   not confident

_____

_____

Name: _____ Date: _____

Directions: Set up the materials to retest your hand pollinator. Look at the picture from Week 2 Day 5 for a reminder. Write the goal you set for the redesign. Then, test your new hand pollinator. Record the results. Answer the questions.

My Redesign Goal

_____

_____

Retest Results

Use color to draw the amount of pollen you see in Cup B.	Write your observations in words.

Look back at your results from the first test. Compare the results.

1. I observed more pollen in Cup B after the retest.

True　　　　　False

2. Did your new design meet the goal you set? Explain why or why not.

_____

_____

Name: _____ Date: _____

Directions: Compare your hand pollinator designs in the Venn diagram. Compare how they looked and how they worked. Then, answer the questions.

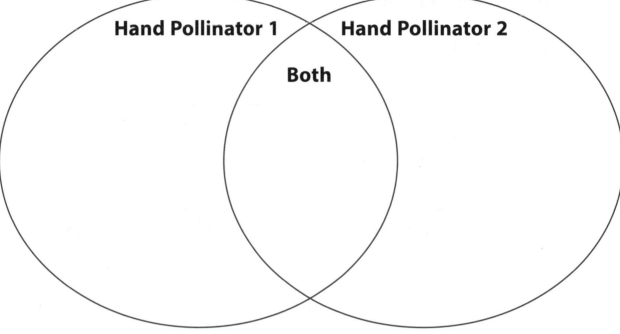

Hand Pollinator 1   **Hand Pollinator 2**

Both

1. What did you learn during this challenge?

_____

_____

2. What did you enjoy about the challenge?

_____

_____

 Try This!

Share your design with others!
Answer any questions they have.

Erosion Teaching Support

Overview of Unit Activities

Students will learn about and explore the effects of wind and water erosion through the following activities:

- reading about and studying images of water erosion
- reading about and studying images of wind erosion
- experimenting with how moving and still water erode candy
- drawing landforms that are shaped by wind over time
- analyzing a diagram of a windbreak
- creating windbreaks to protect homes

Materials Per Group

Week 1

- color-coated candy (3)
- plastic cups (3)
- water (1–2 cups, 250–500 mL)

STEAM Challenge

- basic school supplies
- cotton balls (10+)
- foil pan
- moist sand (3–4 cups, 1 L)
- paper or plastic cup (large)
- ruler or measuring tape
- toothpicks (5–10)
- various natural materials to be used as windbreak (twigs, moss, leaves, burlap, rocks)

Setup and Instructional Tips

- **STEAM Challenge:** The challenge can be done individually or in groups. If students are working in groups, have students sketch their own designs first. Then, have them share their designs in groups and choose one together.

- **Testing Days:** You may choose to do a control test as a group to see how much sand would blow away with no windbreak. Simply set up the sand dune (pile of sand), and blow the fan on it for 20 seconds.

- **Testing Days:** You may wish to have students record their measurements in metric units.

Discussion Questions

- What are weathering and erosion?
- What causes the most erosion?
- What problems can be caused by erosion?
- How can people prevent erosion?
- What are windbreaks, and how are they useful?

Additional Notes

- **Possible Misconception:** Weathering and erosion are the same thing.
  Truth: Weathering is the breaking down of something, such as rock. Erosion is when the smaller pieces are carried away and deposited somewhere else.

- **Possible Design Solutions:** Students may place materials in front or on top of the sand dune. They may have more than one row of shielding materials.

Scaffolding and Extension Suggestions

- Have students research famous sand dune disasters, such as the one that covered houses in Singapore, Michigan.
- Challenge students to use only natural materials that they can find.

Answer Key

Week 1 Day 1
1. C
2. A
3. B

Week 1 Day 2
1. A
2. Example: The rock shape was formed by wind. The wind blew against the rock for millions of years. The wind may have blown harder near the bottom. Or the rock type at the bottom was easier to break down and carry away.

Week 1 Day 5
1. 10–15 mph
2. 100 feet
3. They lower the wind speed near the house. They keep soil from being blown away. They keep snow from piling up too close.

Weeks 2 & 3
See STEAM Challenge Rubric on page 221.

Name: _____ **Date:** _____

Directions: Read the text. Study the picture. Then, answer the questions.

Earth is covered in rocks. There are many different rock types, sizes, and shapes. Most rocks are hard. But over time, they can change. They can be broken down. Water can change their shapes and sizes. It can move them to new places. Waves can crash against rocks and break off pieces. The water carries the pieces to new places. The pieces get smaller and smaller. They become sand.

Water in rivers can carve through rocks. Rivers change the shape of the land. They wash away bits of rock from its bottom and sides. This can make canyons.

1. Over time, waves break down rocks into _____.

   Ⓐ rivers   Ⓒ sand

   Ⓑ boulders   Ⓓ cliffs

2. What caused the formation of the Grand Canyon?

   Ⓐ moving water in a river   Ⓒ animals in the area

   Ⓑ moving water in the   Ⓓ people in the area
      ocean

3. Waves break off pieces of rocks. What happens next?

   Ⓐ They grow bigger.   Ⓒ They become stone.

   Ⓑ Water carries the   Ⓓ Deep canyons are
      pieces away.   formed.

Name: _____ Date: _____

Directions: Read the text. Study the pictures. Then, answer the questions.

Wind can also change the size and shape of rocks. When rocks are broken down by water or wind, it is called *weathering*. When the smaller pieces are carried away, it is called *erosion*.

Wind blows against rocks and mountains. It breaks off small rocks and carries them away. This can make some amazing shapes in the land.

Sand dunes are formed by wind. Sand is carried by wind and left in mounds.

Weathering and erosion by wind has created many unique shapes.

1. Sand dunes are formed by _____ erosion.

    (A) wind   (C) ice

    (B) water   (D) rock

2. Choose one of the three images of landforms created by wind. Write what you think happened to make the land that shape.

_____

_____

Name: _____ Date: _____

Directions: Follow the steps to test how water erodes candy. Then, answer the question.

1. Will moving water or still water cause more erosion? Tell a friend your prediction.

2. Get three clear cups. Fill two of them halfway with water.

3. Place a coated candy in each cup. Record your observations in the chart.

4. Swirl one cup gently for 20 seconds. Do not move the other cups.

5. Repeat step four every 2 or 3 minutes for 20 minutes.

6. Observe the candies. Record any changes.

	No Water	Still Water	Moving Water
Beginning Observations			
Observations After 20 Minutes			

1. Was your prediction correct? What is your evidence?

_____

_____

Day 4

Name: _____ Date: _____

Directions: Draw the stages of a large rock that is eroded by wind. Show how it changes over time.

	This is what the rock looks like after 100 years of wind erosion.

This is what the rock looks like after 1,000 years of wind erosion.	This is what the rock looks like after millions of years of wind erosion.

Name: _____ Date: _____

Directions: Read the text. Study the diagram. Then, answer the questions.

Wind can also erode soil. This can be a problem for people, especially farmers. They need to protect their soil. One way to do that is with a windbreak. Trees are planted in the path of wind. This slows it down. It also keeps snow from piling up.

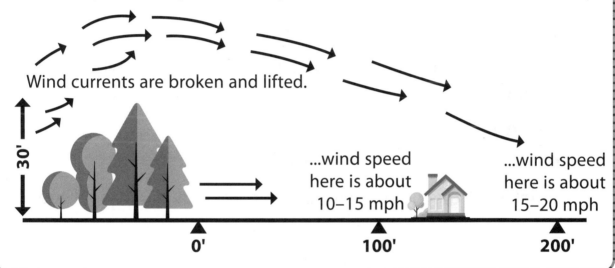

When open wind speed is 35 mph...

Wind currents are broken and lifted.

30'

...wind speed here is about 10–15 mph

...wind speed here is about 15–20 mph

0'   100'   200'

1. You are in the house. The open wind speed is 35 mph.

   What is the windspeed right outside the house? _____

2. How far are the trees from the house? _____

3. How are windbreaks helpful to homes and farms?

   _____

   _____

   _____

Name: _____ Date: _____

Directions: Read the text. Then, answer the question.

The Challenge

Your friend lives near the coast. There are sand dunes nearby. There is a windstorm coming. Their house is at risk of being covered in sand. Build a windbreak to keep the sand from blowing away.

Criteria

To be successful, your windbreak must…

- prevent or reduce the erosion of a pile of sand when a fan blows on it.

Constraints

- You may only use the materials provided to you.

- Ask your teacher how much time you have. Write it here:

_____

Check for Understanding

1. What questions do you need to ask?

_____

_____

_____

_____

Name: _____ **Date:** _____

Directions: Think about what you have learned about wind erosion. Answer questions to help you think of ideas for your windbreak. Then, write any other research questions you have. Search for answers in books or online. Write the answers you find.

1. Where would you place your windbreak on the sand dune?

_____

_____

2. What shapes and sizes might work best to block wind?

_____

_____

3. How could you arrange your windbreak so it does not fall over?

_____

_____

Other Questions I Want to Research	Answers

Name: _____ Date: _____

Directions: Sketch your windbreak design. Draw the sand dune. Show where the windbreak will go. List the materials you will use.

Materials

_____   _____

_____   _____

_____   _____

Name: _____ **Date:** _____

Directions: Look at your design. Complete the checklist as you prepare and build your windbreak.

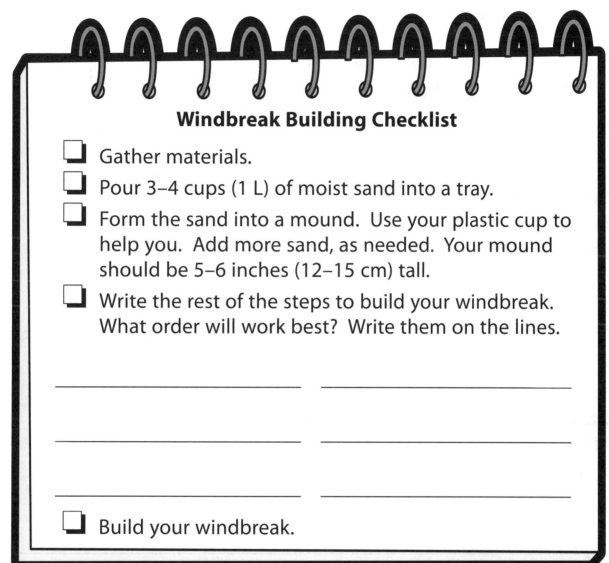

Windbreak Building Checklist

❑ Gather materials.

❑ Pour 3–4 cups (1 L) of moist sand into a tray.

❑ Form the sand into a mound. Use your plastic cup to help you. Add more sand, as needed. Your mound should be 5–6 inches (12–15 cm) tall.

❑ Write the rest of the steps to build your windbreak. What order will work best? Write them on the lines.

_____   _____

_____   _____

_____   _____

❑ Build your windbreak.

Day 5

Name: _____ Date: _____

Directions: Record the height of the sand dune before testing. Set a fan a few feet from your windbreak design. Turn it on low for 20 seconds. Record your observations again.

	Height of Sand Dune	Drawing of Sand Dune
Observations Before Blowing Wind		
Observations After Blowing Wind		

1. Do you think more sand would have been blown away without your windbreak? What is your evidence?

_____

_____

_____

Name: _____ **Date:** _____

Directions: Think about your windbreak design. Answer the questions. Then, plan how you want to improve it.

1. What did you learn from building and testing your first windbreak?

   _____

   _____

2. What new ideas do you want to try?

   _____

   _____

Draw a star next to one or more ways you will improve your windbreak.

- In the first test, the height of the sand dune changed by

  _____ inches.
  My goal is to keep the height change under _____ inches.

- Make a bigger sand dune, and change the windbreak to work with it.

- My own idea: _____

  _____

Name: _____ Date: _____

Directions: Sketch two new windbreak designs. Draw a star next to your favorite. Answer the question.

Redesign 1	**Redesign 2**

1. Why do you think your new design will work better?

_____

_____

Name: _____ **Date:** _____

Directions: Look at your design. Complete the checklist as you prepare and rebuild your windbreak.

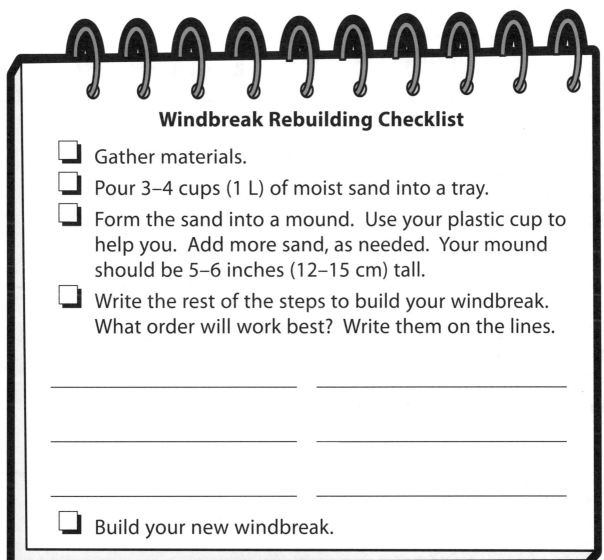

Windbreak Rebuilding Checklist

☐ Gather materials.

☐ Pour 3–4 cups (1 L) of moist sand into a tray.

☐ Form the sand into a mound. Use your plastic cup to help you. Add more sand, as needed. Your mound should be 5–6 inches (12–15 cm) tall.

☐ Write the rest of the steps to build your windbreak. What order will work best? Write them on the lines.

_____   _____

_____   _____

_____   _____

☐ Build your new windbreak.

Name: _____ Date: _____

Directions: Record the height of the sand dune before testing. Set a fan a few feet from your windbreak design. Turn it on low for 20 seconds. Record your observations again.

	Height of Sand Dune	**Drawing of Sand Dune**
Observations Before Blowing Wind		
Observations After Blowing Wind		

1. How did you plan to improve your design?

   _____

   _____

2. Does your new windbreak work better? Write details to explain how you know.

   _____

   _____

Day 5

Name: _____ **Date:** _____

Directions: Think about how you worked on this challenge. Draw yourself as an engineer. Show how you worked on different parts of this challenge.

This is me planning.	This is me building.
This is me testing.	This is me solving a problem.

 Talk About It!

What surprised you about this challenge?

Maps Teaching Support

Overview of Unit Activities

Students will learn about and explore Earth's features and how they can be shown on maps through the following activities:

- reading about and studying pictures of different types of maps
- reading about and studying map keys
- experimenting with making different landforms
- drawing treasure maps
- analyzing a map of South America
- creating puzzle maps

Materials Per Group

Week 1

- modeling clay (green, blue, brown)

STEAM Challenge

- basic school supplies
- cardboard square or poster board (1–2)
- construction paper (assorted colors)
- craft foam (2–4 sheets)
- craft sticks (10–15)
- modeling clay (different earth colors)
- pipe cleaners (5–10)

Setup and Instructional Tips

- **STEAM Challenge:** The challenge works best individually or with partners. If students are working in groups, have students sketch their own designs first. Then, have them share designs in groups and choose one together.

Discussion Questions

- What are some ways maps help us?
- What are the different types of maps?
- Which landforms are shown on maps?
- Which human-made features are shown on maps?
- Why is it important to learn to read maps?
- How do you make a map?

Additional Notes

- **Possible Misconception:** Earth is flat like maps we use.
  Truth: Earth is a sphere, like a globe. Flat maps are easier to use.

- **Possible Design Solutions:** Students may use craft sticks as their puzzle pieces. They can place them on a few pieces of tape while drawing their maps to keep them together. Students might draw their own puzzle pieces on cardboard. They may draw their maps before cutting the pieces.

Scaffolding and Extension Suggestions

- Support students in designing puzzles by having them start with puzzles that have 4–6 square pieces.

- Challenge students to make puzzles with irregular shapes or three-dimensional parts.

Answer Key

Week 1 Day 1
1. B
2. A
3. A

Week 1 Day 2
Venn diagram
Left Side: highest elevation, capital, city, town, highway, railroad, airport, national park
Both: mountains, river, symbols are simple
Right Side: forest, swampland, beach, grove, cave, gumdrop swamp, mountain, lake

Week 1 Day 5
1. You can find deserts on the west coast.

Weeks 2 & 3
See STEAM Challenge Rubric on page 221.

Day 1

Name: _____   Date: _____

Directions: Read the text. Study the pictures. Then, answer the questions.

Maps are helpful. They can be fun, too. Maps can show where land and water are. Some maps show where streets and buildings are. They can show us where to go. They can even tell us if there are many cars on the road. Amusement parks have maps, too. They show where all the rides are. Look at these maps. What can you learn from each one?

Map A	Map B	Map C

1. Which map would be best to use if you need directions home?

   Ⓐ Map A

   Ⓑ Map B

   Ⓒ Map C

   Ⓓ all of the above

2. Which map would best help you know the name of the nearest ocean?

   Ⓐ Map A

   Ⓑ Map B

   Ⓒ Map C

   Ⓓ all of the above

3. Look at the amusement park map. Find the Ferris wheel. Which direction would you go to get to the roller coaster?

   Ⓐ north

   Ⓑ south

   Ⓒ east

   Ⓓ west

Name: _____ **Date:** _____

Directions: Read the text. Study the pictures. Then, compare and contrast the map keys.

Some maps can show details about Earth's surface. They show different landforms. Mountains and rivers are landforms. So are lakes, islands, and valleys. Maps can also show human-made things. They show where cities and roads are. The person who makes the map draws the symbols. Here are two different map keys.

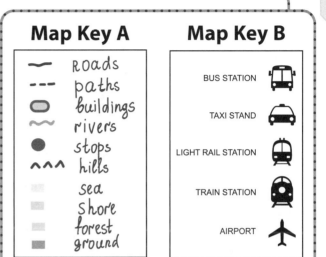

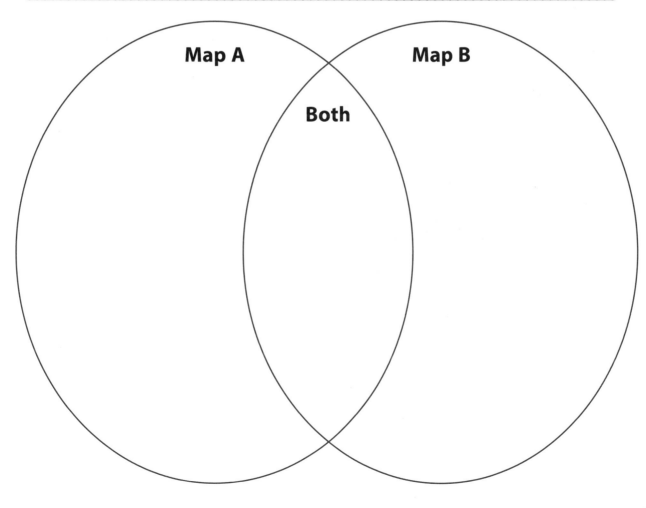

Map A

Map B

Both

Day 3

Name: _____ Date: _____

Directions: Use modeling clay to make models of these landforms. Then, draw a map key symbol for each one.

Landform	Map Key Symbol
island 	
river 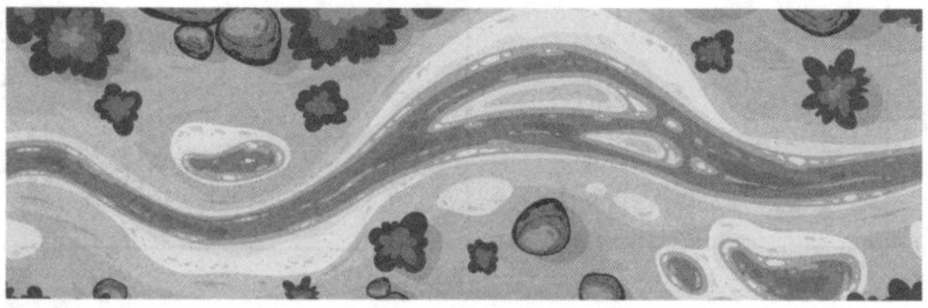	
mountain 	
peninsula 	
plateau 	
lake 	

Name: _____ **Date:** _____

Directions: Design your own treasure map. Draw different landforms. Draw some obstacles. Make a dotted line from the start to finish. Put an *X* where the treasure can be found. Then, label the landforms or areas on your map with fun names.

Name: _____ Date: _____

Directions: Study the map. Then, answer the questions.

South America

Amazon Rain Forest

Andes Mountains

The Pampas

Atlantic Ocean

Pacific Ocean

■	deserts
	grasslands
	tropical forests
△	mountain ranges

1. Where can you find deserts in South America?

_____

2. What part or parts of South America would you like to visit most? Why?

_____

_____

Talk About It!

What other information can you learn from this map?

Name: _____ Date: _____

Directions: Read the text. Then, answer the question.

The Challenge

Puzzles are a great learning tool. Design a puzzle of a map to teach about maps and landforms. It can be of any place, real or pretend. It should have different landforms.

Criteria

To be successful, your map puzzle must…

- have pieces that fit together to make a puzzle.
- have three or more landforms.
- be neat and colorful.

Constraints

- You may only use the materials provided to you.
- Ask your teacher how much time you have. Write it here:

_____

Check for Understanding

1. What questions do you need to ask?

_____

_____

_____

_____

Name: _____ Date: _____

Directions: Find examples of different puzzles. Look for puzzle maps. Look for homemade puzzles. Write or draw ideas you like in the chart. Add your own ideas. Discuss your ideas with others.

Puzzle Piece Shapes and Sizes	Whole Puzzle Shapes and Sizes
Homemade Puzzle Ideas	**Unique or Fun Ideas**

Think About It!

What will you use to make your puzzle pieces? You could use craft sticks. You could cut out pieces of cardboard.

Name: _____ **Date:** _____

Directions: Sketch your puzzle map. Show how the pieces will fit together. Label the landforms. List the materials you will use. Complete the sentence with a number.

Materials

_____   _____

_____   _____

_____   _____

1. My puzzle will have _____ pieces.

Name: _____ Date: _____

Directions: Gather your materials. Plan your steps. Build your puzzle map. Record any changes you make while building.

Think About It!

What order will work best to build your puzzle? If you are cutting the pieces yourself, when should you do that?

Steps to Build My Puzzle Map

_____   _____

_____   _____

_____   _____

Changes Made While Building	Reason for Changes

Name: _____ **Date:** _____

Directions: Ask two or three people to solve your puzzle. Time how long it takes. Ask each tester if they have any feedback. Mark the criteria that were successful.

Tester	Puzzle Time	Feedback

My puzzle map…

❑ has pieces that fit together to make a puzzle.

❑ has three or more landforms.

❑ is neat and colorful.

Unit 10: Maps

Name: _____ Date: _____

Directions: Think about your puzzle map. Answer the questions. Then, plan how you want to improve it.

1. What part of your puzzle do you like best?

_____

2. Draw two puzzle map designs that you saw from others. Put a checkmark by your favorite.

Design 1	Design 2

Draw a star next to one or more ways you will improve your puzzle map.

- My design did not meet the criteria. I will improve it by

_____

_____

- Make the puzzle three-dimensional.
- Make the puzzle double-sided.
- My own idea: _____

_____

Day 2

Name: _____ **Date:** _____

Directions: Plan your new puzzle map design. Then, sketch your new design. Circle any parts or materials that are different or new.

In my redesign, I will…

add _____

remove _____

change _____

Unit 10: Maps

Name: _____ Date: _____

Directions: Gather your materials. Plan your steps. Rebuild your puzzle map. Record any changes you make while building.

Think About It!

What new materials do you need? How do you need to change your steps?

Steps to Rebuild My Puzzle Map

_____   _____

_____   _____

_____   _____

Changes Made While Building	Reason for Changes

Name: _____ Date: _____

Directions: Ask two or three people to solve your puzzle. Time how long it takes. Ask each tester if they have any feedback. Mark the criteria that were successful.

Tester	Puzzle Time	Feedback

My puzzle map…

☐ has pieces that fit together to make a puzzle.

☐ has three or more landforms.

☐ is neat and colorful.

☐ redesign goal was _____

_____

Name: _____ Date: _____

Directions: Think about how you worked on this challenge. Answer the questions.

1. What did you learn during this challenge?

_____

_____

2. What are you most proud of about this challenge?

_____

_____

3. What would you do differently next time?

_____

_____

4. Kids will be excited to play with this puzzle because

_____

_____

Talk About It!

What was the hardest part of this challenge? How did you overcome it or persevere?

Water Cycle Teaching Support

Overview of Unit Activities

Students will learn about and explore the water cycle through the following activities:

- reading about and studying images of the amount of fresh and salt water on Earth
- reading about and studying a diagram of the water cycle
- creating models of how water moves across land
- writing stories about the adventures of a raindrop
- analyzing a graph of average rainfall in different cities
- creating rain chains

Materials Per Group

Week 1

- blue, water-soluble marker
- spray bottle with water

STEAM Challenge

- basic school supplies
- beads
- empty containers (tin or plastic)
- paper clips (20–30)
- plastic spoons (10–20)
- metal craft rings (optional)
- small plastic cups (5–10)
- string or fishing line (2–3 feet, 1 m)
- water (1 cup, 250 mL)

Setup and Instructional Tips

- **STEAM Challenge:** The challenge can be done individually or in groups. If students are working in groups, have students sketch their own designs first. Then, have them share designs in groups and choose one together.
- **Testing Days:** Have students go outside to test their rain chains to avoid a slippery mess.

Discussion Questions

- Where is all the water on Earth located?
- Where is most of the fresh water located?
- What is the water cycle?
- How do we use water in our daily lives?
- What different types of precipitation are there?

Additional Notes

- **Possible Design Solutions:** Students may attach paper clips and/or string to make the lengths of their rain chains. They may add cups or other materials to their chains.

Scaffolding and Extension Suggestions

- Challenge students to design rain chains made only of recycled materials.

Answer Key

Week 1 Day 1

1. A
2. C
3. C

Week 1 Day 2

1. It forms clouds.
2. Example: The sun is what heats the water and causes it to evaporate. Without that heat, the water cycle would not work.
3. Water droplets get heavier and fall back to Earth.

Week 1 Day 5

1. January, February, March
2. September
3. Answers should explain why students would want to visit Cape Town or Tamarindo, based on rainfall.

Weeks 2 & 3

See STEAM Challenge Rubric on page 221.

Name: _____ Date: _____

Directions: Read the text. Study the diagram. Then, answer the questions.

Most of Earth is covered in water. Most of that water is found in the ocean. It is salt water. There is very little fresh water. Fresh water can be found in rivers, lakes, and streams. It can also be found underground. Most fresh water is frozen in ice caps and glaciers. That does not leave much left for drinking.

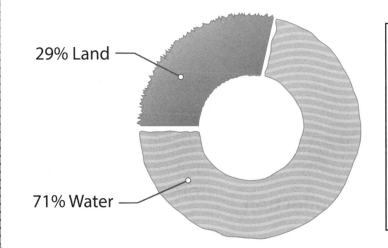

29% Land

71% Water

Earth's water

97% is salt water

3% is fresh water

Less than 1% is drinkable water

1. Where is most of Earth's water found?

(A) in the oceans   (C) in glaciers

(B) underground   (D) in rivers

2. How much water on Earth is fresh water?

(A) 97%   (C) 3%

(B) 71%   (D) 1%

3. Where is most of Earth's fresh water found?

(A) in the oceans   (C) in glaciers and ice caps

(B) in rivers and lakes   (D) on land

Name: _____ Date: _____

Directions: Read the text. Study the diagram. Then, answer the questions.

The water on Earth now is all there will ever be. Earth's water is always moving and changing. It moves through the water cycle.

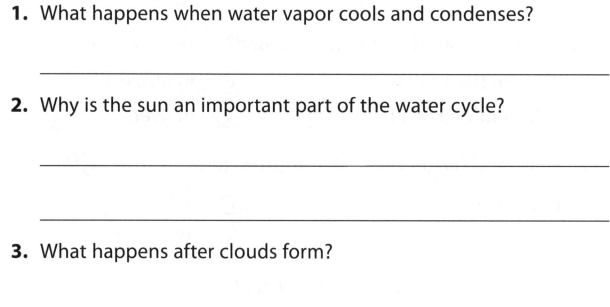

Precipitation
Water droplets get heavier. They fall back to Earth as rain and snow.

Condensation
Water vapor cools and condenses. It forms clouds.

Evaporation
Heat from the sun causes water to evaporate. It changes from a liquid to a gas.

runoff

groundwater

collection

1. What happens when water vapor cools and condenses?

_____

2. Why is the sun an important part of the water cycle?

_____

_____

3. What happens after clouds form?

_____

_____

Name: _____ **Date:** _____

Directions: When it rains in the mountains, where does the water go next? Follow the steps to model how rainwater moves through the water cycle.

1. Crumple a sheet of paper. Then, open it back up. Do not flatten it all the way.

2. You just made mountains! The highest parts of the paper are mountain ridges. The low parts are the valleys. Trace the ridges of your mountains in blue marker.

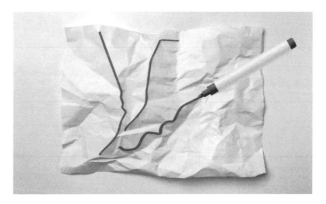

3. Get a spray bottle of water. Spray water over your mountains a few times. Then, watch what happens.

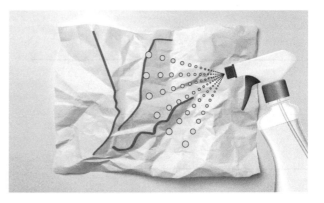

 Talk About It!

Let your paper dry for a few minutes. What did you notice? Where did the rain move?

Day 4

Name: _____ Date: _____

Directions: Write a story about the adventures of one little raindrop. Tell where it goes and what it sees. Tell how it changes and moves through the water cycle. Draw a picture. Then, share your story.

One Raindrop's Adventure

_____

_____

_____

_____

_____

_____

_____

_____

_____

_____

_____

Name: _____ Date: _____

Directions: Read the text. Study the graph. Then, answer the questions.

This graph shows the average rainfall in two different cities.

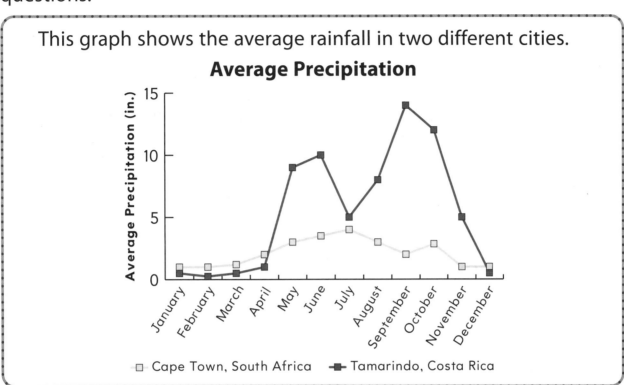

1. During which whole months did Cape Town get more rain than Tamarindo?

   _____

2. In which month did Tamarindo get the most rain?

   _____

3. Which city would you rather visit in the month of October? Why?

   _____

Try This!

Find these two cities on a map or globe. Talk about why you think they have different amounts of rainfall.

Name: _____ Date: _____

Directions: Read the text. Then, answer the question.

The Challenge

Many homes have rain gutters on the roofs. Rain gutters help prevent flooding and water damage. People can add rain chains to help with this. People also like rain chains because they look nice. Build a rain chain to sell at a local home improvement store.

Criteria

To be successful, your rain chain must…

- be at least 3 feet (1 m) long.
- stay together when water is poured at the top.
- be able to hang.

Constraints

- You may only use the materials provided to you.
- Ask your teacher how much time you have. Write it here:

_____

Check for Understanding

1. Write the challenge in your own words.

_____

_____

_____

_____

Name: _____ Date: _____

Directions: Read the text. Look at the examples in the chart. Circle ideas you like.

Rain Chain Designs

Style 1	Style 2
 Many have cup or bowl shapes going from top to bottom.	 They can be made from recycled materials.
Style 3	**Style 4**
 They can be made from natural materials.	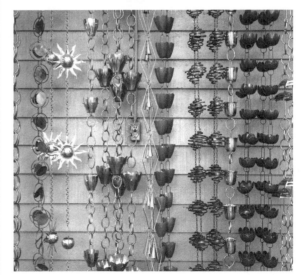 They can have different shapes and colors.

Day 3

Name: _____ Date: _____

Directions: Sketch two designs for your rain chain. Try to make them very different. Circle what you like best in each one. List the materials.

Design 1	Design 2

Materials

_____   _____

_____   _____

_____   _____

Name: _____ Date: _____

Directions: Gather your materials. Plan your steps. Build your rain chain. Record notes as you build.

Steps to Build My Rain Chain

	Steps	Materials Needed
1		
2		
3		
4		
5		
6		

Building Notes
(challenges, surprises, discoveries, changes, etc.)

Name: _____ Date: _____

Directions: Hang your rain chain on a hook outside. Measure it. Pour one cup (250 mL) of water on the top of it. Mark the results in the chart. Ask others for warm and cool feedback. Record their ideas.

Criteria	Circle One	Notes
My rain chain can hang.	yes no	
My rain chain is at least 3 feet (1 m) long.	yes no	
My rain chain stayed together when water was poured at the top.	yes no	

Warm Feedback	**Cool Feedback**
What do they like?	What suggestions do they have?

_____   _____

_____   _____

_____   _____

_____   _____

Name: _____ Date: _____

Directions: Think about your rain chain design. Answer the questions. Then, plan how you want to improve it.

1. What do you want to keep about your rain chain?

   _____

   _____

2. What do you think you need to change to make it better?

   _____

   _____

3. Do you make to make your rain chain bigger?   yes   no

4. Do you need to make your rain chain stronger?   yes   no

Draw a star next to one or more ways you will improve your rain chain.

- My design did not meet the criteria. I will improve it by

  _____

  _____

- Make it longer.
- Add a part that moves when water pours down it.
- My own idea: _____

  _____

Name: _____ Date: _____

Directions: Plan your new rain chain design. Then, sketch your new design. Circle any parts or materials that are different or new.

In my redesign, I will…

add _____

remove _____

change _____

Name: _____ **Date:** _____

Directions: Gather your materials. Plan your steps. Rebuild your rain chain. Record notes during and after you build.

 Think About It!

> What new materials do you need? How do you need to change your steps?

Steps to Rebuild My Rain Chain

	Steps	Materials Needed
1		
2		
3		
4		
5		
6		

Building Notes
(challenges, surprises, discoveries, changes, etc.)

Name: _____ Date: _____

Directions: Retest your rain chain. Mark the results in the chart. Then, answer the questions.

Criteria	Circle One		Notes
My rain chain can hang.	yes	no	
My rain chain is at least 3 feet (1 m) long.	yes	no	
My rain chain stayed together when water was poured at the top.	yes	no	

My Redesign Goals

1. In my design, I wanted to _____

   _____

2. Does your new rain chain meet your redesign goals? Write details to explain how you know.

   _____

   _____

   _____

Day 5

Name: _____ **Date:** _____

Directions: Think about how you worked on this challenge. Answer the questions.

1. What are you most proud of about this challenge?

_____

_____

2. Draw something you enjoyed. Write a caption.	3. Draw your rain chain being used. Write a caption.

 Talk About It!

Try out your rain chain! Find a place to hang it. Even if it is not at the end of a rain gutter, it can still look nice.

Volcanoes Teaching Support

Overview of Unit Activities

Students will learn about and explore the parts of volcanoes and how they erupt through the following activities:

- reading about and studying a diagram about how volcanoes form and erupt
- reading about and studying images of different types of volcanoes
- experimenting with lemon volcanoes
- writing creative stories about why volcanoes form and erupt
- analyzing a map of volcano locations
- creating volcano model party hats

Materials Per Group

Week 1

- baking soda (1 tbsp, 10 g)
- craft stick
- dish soap (1 tsp, 5 mL)
- food coloring (a few drops)
- lemon
- measuring spoon
- plate or bowl for the lemon volcano to "erupt" on

STEAM Challenge

- basic school supplies
- construction paper (various colors)
- cotton balls (5–10)
- tissue paper (volcano colors; 1–2 of each)
- yarn and/or ribbon (volcano colors)

Setup and Instructional Tips

- **Week 1 Day 3:** The lemon volcano eruption can be done by the teacher as a model first. If you choose, students can recreate the eruption on their own.
- **STEAM Challenge:** The challenge can be done individually or in groups. Smaller groups are recommended. If students are working in groups, have students sketch their own designs first. Then, have them share designs in groups and choose one together.

Discussion Questions

- How do volcanoes form?
- Where do volcanoes form?
- What dangers can volcanoes present to humans?
- What are the parts of volcanoes?
- Should people be allowed to live near volcanoes?

Additional Notes

- **Possible Misconception:** Volcanoes are only found on land.
  Truth: Volcanoes can form on the ocean floor as well, especially at plate boundaries.

- **Possible Design Solutions:** Students may make hats shaped like volcanoes and attach them with yarn or by creating head rings with paper. Paper or ribbon might be placed at the top to show eruptions.

Scaffolding and Extension Suggestions

- Support students by modeling how to roll paper at an angle to create cone shapes.

- Challenge students to create volcano party hats that are models of specific volcanoes that students must research and learn about.

Answer Key

Week 1 Day 1
1. B
2. D
3. A

Week 1 Day 2
1. Mount St. Helens is a composite volcano. It is shaped like a tall mountain. It is very big and has steep sides.

Week 1 Day 5
1. Most volcanoes are located at or near plate boundaries. They are near the edges of continents.
2. The east coast of North America does not have volcanoes because there are no plate boundaries there.

Weeks 2 & 3
See STEAM Challenge Rubric on page 221.

Day 1

Name: _____ Date: _____

Directions: Read the text. Study the diagram. Then, answer the questions.

Earth is broken into large pieces. These pieces are called *plates*. They fit together like a puzzle. Volcanoes are often found where Earth's plates meet. A volcano is an opening in Earth's surface. Hot gas and magma can rise through these cracks. Magma is the hot, melted rock under Earth's surface. As it rises, pressure builds. It causes the volcano to erupt. When magma reaches the surface, it is called *lava*. Lava cools and forms into solid rock.

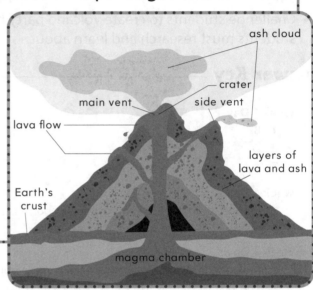

1. Where does magma come from?

   Ⓐ the ocean

   Ⓑ under Earth's surface

   Ⓒ the Earth's atmosphere

   Ⓓ lava flows

2. Earth is broken into _____.

   Ⓐ lava

   Ⓑ volcanoes

   Ⓒ vents

   Ⓓ plates

3. What forms above a volcano when it erupts?

   Ⓐ an ash cloud

   Ⓑ the crust

   Ⓒ a side vent

   Ⓓ a magma chamber

Name: _____ Date: _____

Directions: There are different types of volcanoes. The chart shows three of the main types. Read the text. Study the pictures. Then, answer the question.

Type	Description	Example
cinder cone	These volcanoes have one vent. They are shaped like cones. They have a bowl-shaped crater at the top. They do not get very tall. They are made of cinders of lava. These cinders fall from the sky after an eruption.	Capulin Volcano, New Mexico
composite volcano	These volcanoes grow into tall mountains. They have steep sides. They are made of layers of lava and ash. They can have eruptions that are violent.	Mt. Fuji, Japan
shield volcano	These volcanoes have gentle slopes. They can be very large. They are made of mostly cooled lava. Lava slowly flows out of the vents.	Sierra Negra Volcano, Galapagos

1. Mount St. Helens is a volcano in the state of Washington. What type of volcano do you think it is? Explain your answer.

_____

_____

_____

Day 3

Name: _____ Date: _____

Directions: Read the text. Follow the steps to make a model volcanic eruption.

Lemon Volcano Eruption

1. Have an adult help you cut a lemon in half.

2. Poke the lemon a few times with a craft stick.

3. Place some drops of food coloring on your lemon.

4. Add a teaspoon (5 mL) of dish soap to the top of your lemon.

5. Add a tablespoon (15 mL) of baking soda to the top of your lemon. Draw what happens.

Try This!

Do you want to make a bigger eruption? Squeeze the other half of the lemon onto the volcano.

Name: _____ **Date:** _____

Directions: Read the text. Then, complete the task.

Long ago, people did not know how volcanoes formed. They told stories to help explain what volcanoes were. Some stories told of angry gods or giants. Today, these stories are thought of as legends.

Task: Write your own legend about volcanoes. Tell how they form or why they erupt.

_____

_____

_____

_____

_____

_____

_____

_____

_____

_____

_____

Name: _____ Date: _____

Directions: Read the text. Study the map. Then, answer the questions.

> Volcanoes often form where Earth's pieces, or plates, meet. The Ring of Fire is an area where many of Earth's plates meet. There are many volcanoes in this area.

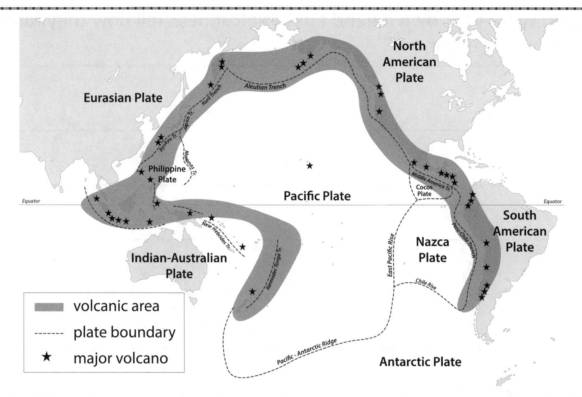

1. What do you notice about where most volcanoes are located?

   _____

   _____

2. Why do you think there are no volcanoes on the east side of North America?

   _____

   _____

Name: _____ **Date:** _____

Directions: Read the text. Then, answer the question.

The Challenge

A local party store wants to offer items with a volcano theme. Help the party store make some designs. Build a party hat for a volcano-themed birthday party.

Criteria

To be successful, your volcano party hat must…

- have the shape of a volcano.
- clearly show at least three parts of a real volcano.
- stay on a student's head while they move around.

Constraints

- You may only use the materials provided to you.
- Ask your teacher how much time you have. Write it here:

_____

Check for Understanding

1. What questions do you need to ask?

_____

_____

_____

_____

Name: _____ Date: _____

Directions: Find examples of party hats or regular hats. Write or draw ideas you like in the chart. Add your own ideas. Discuss your ideas with others. Then, answer the questions.

Shapes	How They Stay in Place
Materials	**Unique or Fun Ideas**

1. What type of volcano will you model with your hat?

   cinder cone   composite volcano   shield volcano

2. What parts of the volcano will you show on your hat?

   _____

   _____

Name: _____ **Date:** _____

Directions: Sketch your volcano party hat. Label the parts of a volcano you will show. List the materials you will use.

Materials

_____   _____

_____   _____

_____   _____

Name: _____ Date: _____

Directions: Plan your steps. Gather your materials. Then, build your volcano party hat. Keep notes as you build.

Steps to Build My Volcano Party Hat

_____   _____

_____   _____

_____   _____

My Building Notes	
Questions	
Challenges	
Changes	

Quick Tip!

It is okay to do a few mini tests as you build!
Make sure your hat will stay secure.

Name: _____ Date: _____

Directions: Answer questions about your volcano party hat. Share it with others. Tell them about it. Show them how it works. Ask them some questions. Write what they say.

Tell

1. What type of volcano did you model your hat after?

   _____

2. What parts of a volcano did you show on your hat?

   _____

   _____

Show

Put your volcano hat on your head. Walk around the room.

3. Did your hat stay on your head?

   yes   no

Ask

4. What do you like?

   _____

   _____

5. How can I make it better?

   _____

   _____

Name: _____ **Date:** _____

Directions: Think about your volcano party hat. Answer the questions. Then, plan how you want to improve it.

1. What do you like best about your first design?

   _____

   _____

2. What ideas from others did you like or want to try?

   _____

   _____

   Draw a star next to one or more ways you will improve your volcano party hat.

   - My design did not meet the criteria. I will improve it by

     _____

     _____

   - Add at least one moving part.
   - Make the parts of the volcano three-dimensional.
   - Create a second piece of volcano party decor (banner, cake topper, etc.).

   - My own idea: _____

     _____

Name: _____ **Date:** _____

Directions: Plan your new volcano party hat. Then, sketch your new design. Circle any parts or materials that are different or new.

In my redesign, I will…

add _____

remove _____

change _____

Day 3

Name: _____ **Date:** _____

Directions: Plan your steps. Gather your materials. Then, rebuild your volcano party hat. Keep notes as you build.

Steps to Rebuild My Volcano Party Hat

_____   _____

_____   _____

_____   _____

 Quick Tip!

You do not have to start from scratch! Make changes to your first design.

My Building Notes	
Questions	
Challenges	
Changes	

Name: _____ Date: _____

Directions: Answer questions about your volcano party hat. Share it with others. Tell them about it. Show them how it works. Ask them some questions. Write what they say.

Tell

1. What changes did you make to your volcano party hat?

_____

_____

2. Why is your new design better?

_____

_____

Show

Put your volcano hat on your head. Walk around the room.

3. Did your hat stay on your head?

yes   no

Ask

4. What do you like?

_____

_____

5. How can I make it better?

_____

_____

Name: _____ Date: _____

Directions: Think about how you worked on this challenge. Answer the questions.

1. What science concepts were important in this challenge?

   _____

   _____

2. What are you most proud of about this challenge?

   _____

   _____

3. Draw yourself at a volcano-themed party. Show everyone wearing your design.

   [ ]

Talk About It!

What other party themes could you make designs for?
How could the designs also teach science or other subjects in fun ways?

Name: _____ Date: _____

STEAM Challenge Rubric

Directions: Think about the challenge. Score each item on a scale of 4 to 1. Circle your score.

4 = Always   3 = Often   2 = Sometimes   1 = Never

					Teacher Score
I used my materials appropriately. I chose materials I thought would work best.	4	3	2	1	
I was creative. I shared new ideas. I tried new ideas.	4	3	2	1	
I cooperated with others.	4	3	2	1	
I shared my thinking with others.	4	3	2	1	
I recorded my work, observations, and results.	4	3	2	1	
I followed directions.	4	3	2	1	
I persevered.	4	3	2	1	
I worked through the steps of the Engineering Design Process.	4	3	2	1	

Teacher Notes

_____

_____

_____

_____

Name: _____ Date: _____

Summative Assessment

Directions: Answer the questions.

1. An engineer is given a new design challenge. What should they do first?

   (A) start gathering materials for the challenge

   (B) ask questions to make sure they understand the challenge

   (C) find team members to work with on the challenge

   (D) research designs and ideas of others

   Explain your choice: _____

   _____

2. An engineer is someone who _____

   _____

3. You test a paper airplane you made. It does not go very far. What will you do next?

   _____

   _____

4. Why is redesign an important part of the engineering design process?

   _____

   _____

Engineering Design Process

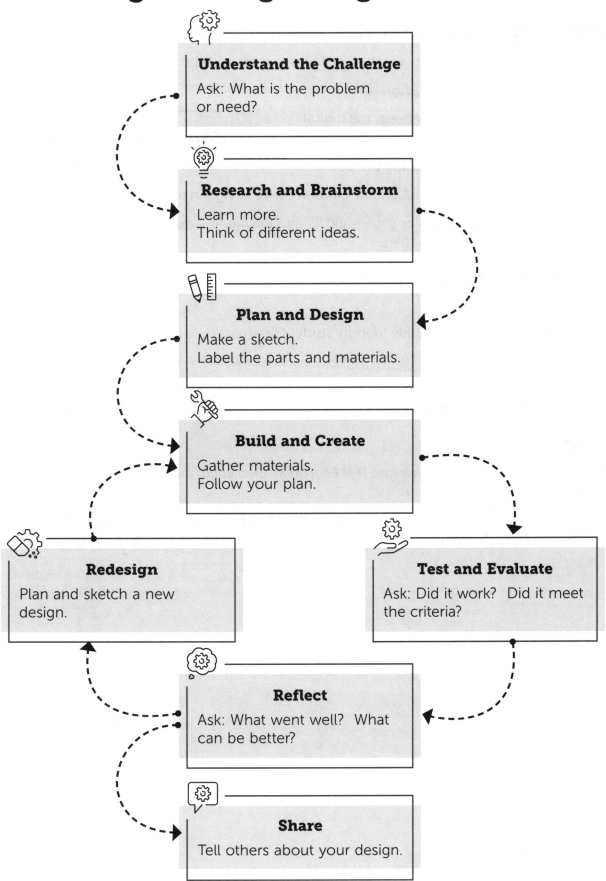

Understand the Challenge

Ask: What is the problem or need?

Research and Brainstorm

Learn more.
Think of different ideas.

Plan and Design

Make a sketch.
Label the parts and materials.

Build and Create

Gather materials.
Follow your plan.

Redesign

Plan and sketch a new design.

Test and Evaluate

Ask: Did it work? Did it meet the criteria?

Reflect

Ask: What went well? What can be better?

Share

Tell others about your design.

Digital Resources

Accessing the Digital Resources

The digital resources can be downloaded by following these steps:

1. Go to **www.tcmpub.com/digital**.

2. Use the ISBN number to redeem the digital resources.

ISBN: 978-1-4258-2529-4

3. Respond to the question using the book.

4. Follow the prompts on the Content Cloud website to sign in or create a new account.

5. Choose the digital resources you would like to download. You can download all the files at once or a specific group of files.

Contents of the Digital Resources

- Safety Contract
- Sentence frames to help guide friendly student feedback
- Materials requests for students' families
- Student Glossary
- Materials list for the whole book

References Cited

Bybee, Rodger W. 2013. *The Case for STEM Education: Challenges and Opportunities.* Arlington, VA: NSTA Press.

NGSS Lead States. 2013. "Next Generation Science Standards: For States, By States APPENDIX I—Engineering Design in the NGSS." Washington, DC.